"Jeremy Pettit and Ryan Hill created a very useful text for y[...]
with adolescents. The book uses evidence-based principle[...]
reader with accessible tools for youth in crisis, or who v[...]
skills. *Overcoming Suicidal Thoughts for Teens* is an absolute must-add to any set of
training resources for clinicians!"

—**Robert Cramer, PhD**, associate professor of public health sciences, and
Irwin Belk Distinguished Scholar in Health Research at UNC Charlotte

"This groundbreaking and timely work will help countless teenagers who are quietly
dealing with internalized feelings of desperation and hopelessness around seemingly
insurmountable pressures in their lives. It is viewed as a much-needed resource for
teenagers to destigmatize the topic of self-harm during a time of unparalleled social
and political unrest, and pressures associated with social media, the hypercompetitive
world of college entrance examinations achievement and advancement, and prolonged
pandemic-related angst and disruption."

—**Gary X. Lancelotta, PhD, ABPP**, board certified in clinical child
and adolescent psychology; and director of Child Psychology Associates,
P.A. in Miami, FL

"Therapists working with suicidal teens will find the Pettit and Hill book valuable in
both guiding their treatment and as a self-help manual for the teens they are treating.
Four different case vignettes run throughout the book, providing opportunities for
teens to see situations that they themselves may have encountered in a new light.
Coping behaviors, and other techniques, employed by the four teens will be useful for
any reader."

—**Anthony Spirito, PhD, ABPP**, professor of psychiatry and human
behavior at the Alpert Medical School of Brown University, who has
conducted treatment research with suicidal teens for over twenty-five years

"*Overcoming Suicidal Thoughts for Teens* is a fantastic resource. It offers practical, specific, down-to-earth skills in a very clear framework with action steps for all levels of
suicidal thinking. It is written in an approachable and matter-of-fact style, and uses
easy-to-understand metaphors that help normalize the experience of having thoughts
of suicide that so many teens experience."

—**Jennifer Battle, MSW**, director of Access at The Harris Center for
Mental Health and IDD; and adjunct faculty at the University of
Houston Graduate College of Social Work

"*Overcoming Suicidal Thoughts For Teens* is an approachable, practical, and compassionate guide filled with science-based strategies from cognitive behavioral therapy (CBT) that can help teens continue living. Jeremy Pettit and Ryan Hill expertly coach readers through coping with challenges, increasing hope and connection, and living a life of purpose and meaning. This book is a fantastic resource not only for teens, but also for their parents and mental health professionals."

> **—Kelly L. Green, PhD**, psychologist and senior research investigator at the Center for the Prevention of Suicide at the University of Pennsylvania

"Given the current mental health crisis among youth in the US, *Overcoming Suicidal Thoughts for Teens* is a timely and much-needed resource. Pettit and Hill provide a variety of practical skills and techniques that are supported by science yet discussed in a manner that young people will understand and find useful. Grounded in research, clinical work, and lived experience, this book will help even the most distressed teenagers overcome their suicidal thoughts and build a life of purpose."

> **—Dorian A. Lamis, PhD, ABPP**, clinical psychologist, and associate professor at the Emory University School of Medicine

"This book is an excellent, much-needed resource for teenagers who experience suicidal thoughts. Written in a way that is clear, engaging, accessible, and nonjudgmental, teens can use this on their own or as a companion to therapy to help them address thoughts, feelings, and stressors that might lead them to think about suicide; improve their relationships; and remind them of their reasons for living."

> **—Regina Miranda, PhD**, professor of psychology at Hunter College and The Graduate Center at CUNY, director of the Youth Suicide Research Consortium, and coeditor of *Handbook of Youth Suicide Prevention*

the *i n s t a n t* h e l p
s o l u t i o n s   s e r i e s

Young people today need mental health resources more than ever. That's why New Harbinger created the **Instant Help Solutions Series** especially for teens. Written by leading psychologists, physicians, and professionals, these evidence-based self-help books offer practical tips and strategies for dealing with a variety of mental health issues and life challenges teens face, such as depression, anxiety, bullying, eating disorders, trauma, and self-esteem problems.

Studies have shown that young people who learn healthy coping skills early on are better able to navigate problems later in life. Engaging and easy-to-use, these books provide teens with the tools they need to thrive—at home, at school, and on into adulthood.

This series is part of the **New Harbinger Instant Help Books** imprint, founded by renowned child psychologist Lawrence Shapiro. For a complete list of books in this series, visit newharbinger.com.

overcoming suicidal thoughts for teens

cbt activities to reduce pain, increase hope & build meaningful connections

JEREMY W. PETTIT, PhD
RYAN M. HILL, PhD

Instant Help Books
An Imprint of New Harbinger Publications, Inc.

Publisher's Note

This publication is designed to provide accurate and authoritative information in regard to the subject matter covered. It is sold with the understanding that the publisher is not engaged in rendering psychological, financial, legal, or other professional services. If expert assistance or counseling is needed, the services of a competent professional should be sought.

INSTANT HELP, the Clock Logo, and NEW HARBINGER are trademarks of New Harbinger Publications, Inc.

New Harbinger Publications is an employee-owned company.

Copyright © 2022 by Jeremy Pettit and Ryan Hill
Instant Help Books
An imprint of New Harbinger Publications, Inc.
5674 Shattuck Avenue
Oakland, CA 94609
www.newharbinger.com

All Rights Reserved

Cover design by Amy Shoup

Acquired by Ryan Buresh

Edited by Kristi Hein

Library of Congress Cataloging-in-Publication Data on file

Printed in the United States of America

24   23   22

10   9   8   7   6   5   4   3   2   1   First Printing

Contents

Acknowledgments

We are indebted to many colleagues who have shaped the ideas in this book. We are grateful to Dr. Rheeda Walker for her words of wisdom and encouragement that influenced the decision to write this book. We are especially grateful to Ryan Buresh and the staff at New Harbinger Publications for their guidance and support throughout its development. Most of all, we are grateful to the young people who have allowed us to walk with them on difficult parts of their journeys. They have inspired us more than they will ever know.

A Note from the Authors

Dear Reader,

We commend you for your courage in selecting this book. The fact that you are reading this probably means that you struggle with thoughts of suicide. Choosing to pick up this book, when thoughts of suicide drag you down, is an act of defiance! It takes courage and strength to choose life when you feel disconnected, hopeless, and worthless. Choosing to keep fighting is evidence of your strength and will to live.

We wrote this book for you. We have dedicated our lives to helping young people who struggle with thoughts of suicide. This book is based on science, clinical experience, and lived experience demonstrating that teens just like you can win the battle against suicidal thoughts. In the following pages, we pass on that knowledge and experience to you, to help you overcome the challenges, traumas, and trials in your life. You are not alone in this struggle. Millions of young people think about suicide, and we have seen many, from all different backgrounds and circumstances, go on to build a life of purpose and connection.

In the following pages you'll learn new skills, gain new insights, and find new ways to view and navigate the world. We'll walk you through each new skill and technique to help guide you on this part of your journey. Of course, not every skill works for every person; that's why we present a range of skills and activities for you to consider. It'll take some trial and error, so be patient and keep going until you find what works for you!

A few words of advice as you proceed through the book: First, grab a notebook or journal and keep it with you throughout this process. We often ask you to write down your thoughts, brainstorm ideas, and make lists. Writing about thoughts and emotions can be therapeutic. It also helps you remember the skills and techniques. By keeping a notebook, you'll have all of your thoughts and skills in one place.

Second, step outside your comfort zone. Try out new skills and give the activities a try. Learning new skills works only if you put them into practice. Some of them may seem a bit silly or feel awkward the first few times—that's okay. We grow the most when we push ourselves out of our comfort zones. Finally, if you stall out, get bogged down, or give up for a few days, that's okay. Just pick up the book and try again! No journey is completed without a few bumps along the way. What is important is that you come back and keep trying.

Above all, keep fighting to live. Continue defying thoughts of suicide. Start building a life that you want, desperately, to live, explore, and experience. Read on—there's no time like the present to get started.

Best wishes on your journey,
Jeremy and Ryan

CHAPTER 1

Preparing for the Journey

You've probably heard the saying, "Life is a journey." On your life's journey, you'll encounter beautiful views that inspire you and take your breath away, grueling climbs that test your strength and resolve, fast downhill descents that simultaneously exhilarate and terrify, and mind-numbingly boring stretches of road that make you question where you're going. It's all part of being alive.

The teenage years often include exciting parts of your journey, but many teens also find that these years include difficult, challenging times. There's a lot of new and unfamiliar terrain in these years—physically, emotionally, socially, romantically, academically, and otherwise. When you're a teen, your body and brain develop and change rapidly; how you relate to others changes, others' expectations of you change, your level of independence from caretakers changes (but maybe not as quickly as you want!), and demands put upon you in school change. So much change in such a short period creates stress! Stress can feel like obstacles on your journey, making it hard to move forward. Finding your way through these changes and obstacles can feel overwhelming at times.

It's no surprise, then, that many teens struggle with negative feelings like sadness, anger, and fear, and with thoughts of suicide. When obstacles are in your way, it's normal to experience negative feelings and question whether to continue your journey. As you'll read later in this chapter, lots of teens ask themselves this question when they experience difficult parts of their journeys. And even though the teen years are characterized by change and stress, sometimes it's hard to figure out why you're having suicidal thoughts and where they come from.

There's a bright side: many people experience a calmer, more fulfilling stretch of their journey after passing through the challenges and unfamiliar terrain of the teen years. Also, as your body and brain mature, and as you learn from your experiences navigating the rocky terrain of the teen years, you become better equipped to handle future difficulties in your journey. So the journey typically gets smoother in adulthood. On the not-so-bright side, every life journey encounters difficult and stressful times; it's just that your teen years can be particularly hard to navigate. That's why it's important to have all the information and skills you need to face this part of your journey. This book will help you identify the right gear to pack so you can handle whatever terrain you are facing right now and whatever lies ahead.

In a later section, you'll work on identifying the right gear. Before doing that, though, it's important to understand that you're not alone on your journey.

A SHARED JOURNEY

Many teens believe they're the only one having suicidal thoughts. That can be a lonely feeling! It's also understandable, because in our society we don't talk openly about suicidal thoughts. If nobody's talking about it, it makes sense to assume nobody else is experiencing it, right? But suicidal thoughts are very common, especially among teens. Surveys consistently show that about one in five high school students in the United States has these thoughts every year (Ivey-Stephenson, Demissie, Crosby, et al., 2020). That works out to more than three million high school students every year who seriously think about suicide, not to mention millions of middle school students who experience similar thoughts. So, while your journey is unique to you, know that many other people are also on journeys that include suicidal thoughts. They can relate to some of the things you experience, like emotional pain, loneliness, difficult relationships with others, and thoughts about ending the journey.

Also keep in mind that teens aren't the only ones who experience suicidal thoughts! Many famous adults also experience them. A handful of examples include artists Katy Perry, Nicki Minaj, Eminem, and Demi Lovato; actors Pete Davidson, Halle Berry, and Drew Carey; and athletes Ronda Rousey, Michael Phelps, and Mike Tyson. Think about other famous people who have spoken about their experiences with suicidal thoughts and behaviors (if you can't think of any, Google it!). People in all walks of life experience suicidal thoughts—teachers, politicians, writers, pilots, caregivers, dentists, chefs, computer programmers, and so on.

The point is that experiencing suicidal thoughts is not unusual. Millions experience them every year. As the saying goes, "It's okay to not be okay." But experiencing suicidal thoughts *is* unpleasant, and it can lead to dangerous situations if it isn't addressed. That's why it's important for you to develop skills to effectively cope with suicidal thoughts and find your way to more peace of mind and contentedness on your journey. This book will help! Each chapter covers specific skills to help you cope with suicidal thoughts. The skills you'll learn are based on extensive research with teens like you and real-world experience on how to help teens when they experience suicidal thoughts.

Before introducing those skills, let's make sure you have the right gear for your journey, including this book and a journal to record your thoughts. Throughout this book, we'll ask you to think about things and jot down some of your thoughts, feelings, and plans. Keeping a journal is a good way to express your thoughts and feelings, refresh your memory on tips and strategies you'll learn, and track your progress.

PACKING THE RIGHT GEAR FOR THE JOURNEY

Every journey is different, so each requires different types of gear and equipment. We all experience obstacles—nobody has a problem-free life! You may be able to make it past some obstacles with only your basic gear and equipment: the skills needed to cope with situations and feelings. That's because some obstacles are small and relatively easy to go around, over, or through. For example, you might consider a disagreement with a friend a minor obstacle, and you might navigate around it by telling yourself it isn't a big deal and by reaching out to your friend to patch things up. Or you might feel worried and have trouble sleeping for a couple of days before a test, so you prepare for it by studying, and once it's over you feel better. Simple enough, right?

But suicidal thoughts are big obstacles that try to convince you to end your journey long before it reaches its natural end. Like a boulder in the middle of a mountain pass, suicidal thoughts tell you not to go any further. *Turn back. Quit trying. End your journey here and now.* So dealing with suicidal thoughts requires special gear. Like this book!

You can think of this book like climbing gear. The skills you'll gain to cope with painful emotions and suicidal thoughts are the equipment you'll use to climb over that boulder blocking the route. For example, after an argument with a family member, the thoughts *It would have been better if I had never been born* or *My family would be better off without me* may enter your mind and stay there for a while. Those thoughts often arise from the emotional pain you experience, the hurtful things others say, and your belief that things will never get better. Sometimes ending your life may seem like the only way to escape the pain, especially when you can't see a path toward things getting better in the future. If you have experiences like this, remember that you aren't alone, and know that help is available. There are ways to get over the boulders that block your way. The activities in this book will help you do that by managing these thoughts, coping with the pain you experience, and building stronger relationships with others in your life.

Having said that, other parts of your journey may still require more gear than this book provides. The intensity of your suicidal thoughts may reach a level where you need professional help from a counselor or an acute crisis service, like the Suicide Prevention Lifeline (dial 988) or the Crisis Text Line (text 741741). There is no shame in that—everyone needs help from others at times. The activities in this book are helpful for anyone who thinks about suicide, but if your suicidal thoughts become very intense you'll need to work with a professional to stay safe and manage the distress you are experiencing.

In the rest of this chapter, we'll look at the kinds of suicidal thoughts you might struggle with and the type of support that's most appropriate for you. We'll also explore your other options—counseling, acute crisis services—so you can stay safe and well as you continue your journey.

In the next section, you'll identify times when this book provides what you need to manage thoughts of suicide, and times when you need outside help.

IDENTIFYING THE RIGHT LEVEL OF HELP

A traffic light provides instructions when you're driving: yellow means caution, red means stop and wait, and green means go. You can think of the traffic light scheme as a metaphor to indicate the intensity of your thoughts about suicide and help you identify the right level of help. The figure on the following page shows different types of thoughts you might have, the intensity of each type, and what you can do at each level to get help. The thoughts shown on the left are just examples. You'll learn more about your own thoughts next.

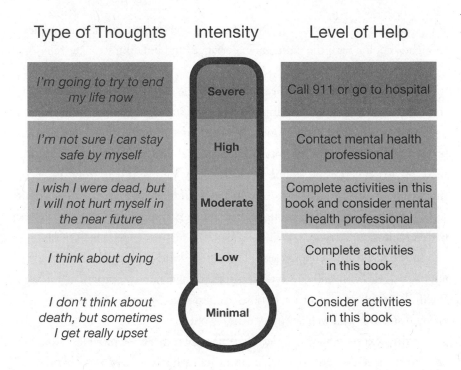

Type of Thoughts	Intensity	Level of Help
I'm going to try to end my life now	Severe	Call 911 or go to hospital
I'm not sure I can stay safe by myself	High	Contact mental health professional
I wish I were dead, but I will not hurt myself in the near future	Moderate	Complete activities in this book and consider mental health professional
I think about dying	Low	Complete activities in this book
I don't think about death, but sometimes I get really upset	Minimal	Consider activities in this book

At the minimal intensity level, you aren't thinking about death. The appropriate level of help is to consider completing the activities in this book, to better prepare yourself to manage occasional upset feelings.

The low level indicates you think sometimes about death, but you don't have thoughts of suicide or hurting yourself. The activities in this book provide the appropriate level of help.

The moderate level indicates you have some thoughts about wanting to be dead, but no plans or intentions to hurt yourself. The appropriate level of help would include completing the activities in this book and considering seeking help from a mental health professional.

The high level indicates you have thoughts about hurting yourself, so you're not sure you can stay safe by yourself. If you have thoughts like this, it's important to reach out for help and contact a mental health professional.

The severe level indicates that you are thinking about ending your life now. These types of thoughts indicate high intensity. If you experience thoughts like these, you should immediately seek help by asking a trusted adult to help you access a crisis intervention service, calling a hotline number like the Suicide Prevention Lifeline (988) or emergency number 911, or going to a hospital.

You may find yourself somewhere in between these levels; they are not really separate levels, but a continuous gradient. If you find yourself in between the levels named in the figure, we recommend you pursue the level of help at the next higher level in the figure to be on the safe side.

In your journal, write down a few of the thoughts you have most often about death or suicide. It can be hard and upsetting to focus on these thoughts and write them down. If you need to, take a break from writing down your thoughts and do something calming, like taking a walk or listening to music, and return to it later. Though it can be upsetting, expressing yourself is helpful in the long run because it allows you to better understand what you think and feel. Better understanding of *what* you think and feel is a step toward better understanding of *why* you think and feel that way. This will help you learn *how* to cope with the painful thoughts and feelings.

Once you have written down your thoughts, return to the figure and ask yourself:

1. *What intensity level best matches my thoughts?*

2. *What should I do based on this intensity level?*

Each of the thoughts you just identified is like a traffic light on your life journey, alerting you to what's ahead and prompting you to take the appropriate action. Later in this chapter, we'll start to explore possible reasons for having these thoughts, which will set the stage for addressing these reasons and reducing your pain. But right now, let's look at some ways you can make sure you stay safe and well.

No matter how intense your thoughts may feel, the skills you'll learn in this book will help you cope with stressful situations, manage painful feelings, and build better relationships. But if your thoughts reach the high or severe levels, the next section in particular will help. We start with these levels because keeping you safe and well is the top priority. When you have suicidal thoughts, it can feel like things will never get better. In reality, things can and do get better—with help. By staying safe and well while you're going through hard parts of your journey, you get to experience what comes next in your life! Connecting with professional help is the best way to do that when you're at high or severe levels. We'll get to the lower intensity levels later.

IDENTIFYING HOW TO GET HELP

Now that you have seen how intense your thoughts are and have identified appropriate levels of help, we'll focus on identifying how to get help. Let's begin with Skyler's story.

Skyler has just turned fifteen. Skyler is an average student in school, getting mostly B's and C's. She's an excellent musician, playing trombone in the school band. She's also pretty good on the piano. Playing music is when Skyler feels most at peace and confident. She knows other kids from band and hangs out with them at lunch and between classes. But Skyler stays mostly on the edges of conversations—she's there in the group but feels like she doesn't really fit in. Sometimes she wonders if her friends would even notice if she weren't there.

At home, Skyler spends most of her time alone in her room, watching videos on the internet and playing music. She feels lonely even though she knows a lot of people. She argues with her caregivers almost daily about seemingly everything. They are always pushing her to make better grades and spend less time on her phone; they don't seem to care that she excels in music. After all, "Playing the trombone won't land you a good-paying job," they say.

Lately, Skyler has been thinking that life is too painful to go on and that dying would be a big relief. She's never shared these thoughts with anyone—she's worried that if people knew she had these thoughts they would think she's weird or crazy and not want to be around her.

What is the intensity level of Skyler's suicidal thoughts?

If you said moderate, you're right! Skyler thinks about dying but doesn't have plans to hurt herself. Think about specific recommendations you could give Skyler to find help. If you were talking with Skyler, what would you recommend she do?

We recommend several possible ways for Skyler to find help: talking to the school counselor about her thoughts, asking her parent to help her find a mental health counselor, and reading this book. If Skyler's thoughts were at a high or severe level, she could call the Suicide Prevention Lifeline (988), text the Crisis Text Line (741741), or ask her parent to take her to the nearest hospital.

Now think about how you could apply these recommendations to your own experiences. In your journal, write down a couple of specific actions you can take if you're ever at a high or severe level, now or in the future. Who can you turn to for the help you need?

If you need more tips, consider searching on the internet for more hotlines and text lines. These have two advantages: they're available at all times, and they connect you with someone who has training in how to help.

It can also help to tell someone you trust about your thoughts and feelings. Like Skyler, many teens are afraid of what other people will think about them if they open up about suicidal thoughts. They worry about being judged by others, labeled as "crazy," or disappointing people in their lives. Those worries are understandable, but they're almost always wrong, especially if their thoughts are shared with a trusted adult. While it can be hard to talk with someone else about personal, sensitive topics like suicidal thoughts, it usually results in staying safe and feeling better.

Have you ever talked with someone about your suicidal thoughts? If so, how did they respond? If not, what has held you back? Sharing your personal and at times intense experiences with someone else can be hard! It makes you vulnerable to negative reactions or even rejection. Some people in your life might want to be helpful but not know how to respond. For example, other teens who are going through similar difficult parts of their journey are usually not in a good position to give you helpful support. Others might feel uncomfortable talking about distressing feelings, so they respond by shutting down or changing the subject. Still others might have trouble understanding what it's like to have suicidal thoughts and respond by minimizing the pain you are experiencing ("It's no big deal; you'll be fine"). But there *are* people who will listen, empathize with what you're experiencing, and provide support and help. So it's important to identify the right people to talk with.

Chapter 2 provides tips and guidance on doing just that, including how to ask for help and a sample letter you could share with your caregiver to ask for their help. To get the wheels turning now, though, go ahead and name an adult or adults in your life whom you could absolutely trust and turn to if you ever needed to. Maybe it's a caregiver, a grandparent, a teacher or coach, or a spiritual advisor. It can be anyone; what matters is that you can trust them and know that they will be there when you need help. Write these in your journal.

Next, how do you know when to reach out for extra help? The following list of thoughts, behaviors, and feelings can help you develop a sense for this. Some of the items might bring up strong feelings for you. It's okay if you need to step away, take deep breaths to soothe yourself, and then return. When you're ready, read through the list and identify any items that are true of you now.

- ☐ Thinking repeatedly and in detail about how to hurt yourself

- ☐ Getting things ready to hurt yourself, like getting pills to take or a belt to hang yourself

- ☐ Actually hurting yourself, like cutting or burning yourself

- ☐ Writing a note telling people good-bye

- ☐ Experiencing long bouts of sadness or worry that don't go away on their own

- ☐ Feeling restless, agitated, and unable to sleep

If any of these items describe you now, it's important for you to get extra help from a professional while you work through this book. Again, there's no shame in needing help! Many teens experience these types of thoughts and need extra help on their journey. Recognizing when you need it and knowing how to find it are signs that you're on the right path.

Many teens wonder what professional help might look like. What images come to mind when you think of professional help for suicidal thoughts? You might think of medications, lying on a couch telling an aloof analyst about your dreams, or being locked in a hospital. While all three could be possibilities (though a good counselor won't be aloof and may want to hear about your waking life, not your dreams), professional help takes different forms and often looks very different from how it's portrayed in movies (you'll find details in chapter 8). It almost always includes talking with a caring person who is trained to help you cope with upset feelings and suicidal thoughts. Often these conversations happen privately between you and the professional, but when you're a minor some of the conversations will include your caregiver. Depending on the specific thoughts and feelings you're experiencing, medication may or may not be recommended.

Deciding whether to take medication will involve you, your caregiver, and a physician. In severe situations where there is concern that you may not be able to stay safe in the short term, you might need to stay in a hospital.

The purposes of any treatment, including hospitalization, are to keep you safe and to reduce the intensity of your suicidal thoughts. For suicidal thoughts in the moderate range, treatments like meeting with a counselor and/or taking medication are typically enough to keep you safe while working to address and cope with whatever triggers your suicidal thoughts. When thoughts are in the severe range, talking with a counselor or taking medication may not be enough to keep you safe. The hospital is there to protect you during the really intense times. Typically, hospital stays are short, from a few days to a week, although they could be shorter or longer depending on the circumstances. During hospital stays, it's common for teens to:

- Talk with counselors about their thoughts, sometimes alone and sometimes in a group of teens who experience similar thoughts

- Participate in activities like art or recreation

- Share meals together with other teens

- Sometimes do schoolwork

Regardless of what form professional help takes for you, what's important is that you're getting help from caring people with special training in how to keep you safe and cope with your suicidal thoughts.

UNDERSTANDING WHAT YOU STRUGGLE WITH—AND WHY

As you have seen in this chapter, thoughts differ in intensity or severity. They also differ in content, meaning what you think about. Sometimes you might think about death or dying, but it isn't suicidal. For example, you might wonder what it's like to be dead or who would come to your funeral if you died. Those aren't really suicidal thoughts. They could be curiosity or philosophical thoughts, or maybe thoughts to try to distract yourself from a difficult situation. But they aren't suicidal, because they aren't about ending your life. And by the way, those types of thoughts are really common!

At other times, you might experience thoughts about suicide that don't involve directly harming yourself. These have sometimes been called *passive thoughts*. Passive is the opposite of active. Passive thoughts occur when you feel like you don't want to be alive but you don't think about taking actions to end your life. For example, you might have a thought such as *I wish I had never been born* when you experience a disappointment like failing a test. Other passive thoughts are *I wish I could go to sleep and never wake up* and *My family would be better off without me.* These thoughts are about your life ending, but they don't involve you taking action to end it. Just because passive suicidal thoughts aren't about ending your life doesn't mean they aren't serious or upsetting. They still hurt on an emotional level, and they can escalate to more dangerous types of thoughts. For these reasons, this book will help you develop skills for coping with them.

At still other times, you might have *active thoughts* about suicide that involve directly harming yourself or taking action to end your life. For example, after a big fight with family members you might have a thought such as *I should shoot myself and end it all now.* Other active thoughts are *Taking a bottle of pills would end my pain* and *I am going to write a good-bye letter to my friends before I kill myself.* Like passive thoughts, active thoughts are emotionally painful, but they also indicate higher risk to your safety and well-being.

Take a few moments to reflect on the kinds of suicidal thoughts you have. In your journal, write down thoughts as they come to your mind. Are they passive, active, or some of both? Starting to recognize and understand the kinds of thoughts you struggle with is a key step toward changing them.

Importantly, understanding what you struggle with can also help you stay safe in the short term by seeking out the appropriate level of help. If you find yourself often having active thoughts—thoughts that might compel you to act on them—it's important to get extra help from a professional while you work through this book.

Whether your thoughts are passive, active, or both, you've probably wondered why you have them. This *why?* is one of the hardest questions to answer in life. Understanding the reasons for some things can be challenging. You might never fully understand why some things happen or why you feel certain ways. But if you pay attention to your thoughts and monitor them, you can gain insight into things that trigger and maintain your suicidal thoughts. That insight is important, because it gives you ideas about how to make things better.

As we've said, focusing on suicidal thoughts can be upsetting. Focusing on the reasons you experience suicidal thoughts can be difficult, too, but it's a necessary step on the path to feeling better and continuing on your journey. No single reason or trigger can explain all suicidal thoughts. Different things trigger suicidal thoughts for different people and at different times. For example, maybe a romantic breakup triggered your suicidal thoughts, but anxiety about doing well in school triggered suicidal thoughts in someone else. Think back to Skyler—what contributed to her suicidal thoughts?

Starting to gain insight into what contributes to your suicidal thoughts will help you address, reduce, and even prevent suicidal thoughts from occurring. The following list includes some of the most common reasons for suicidal thoughts in teenagers. As the list illustrates, there are many different feelings and situations that can lead you to think about suicide. Take a look and see which, if any, of these reasons applies to you.

- Relationship problems

- Hopelessness

- Trauma

- School problems

- Loneliness

- Depression

- Legal problems

- Discrimination

- Anxiety

- Health or sleep problems

- Bullying

- Substance use problems

Are you experiencing any of these now? Can you identify other personally relevant reasons not included on this list? If so, jot them down in your journal so you can keep a list of possible triggers for your suicidal thoughts.

In the next chapter, you'll learn how to recognize and respond to your triggers in healthy ways. For now, focus on developing awareness of the types of thoughts you experience, when you typically experience them, and what triggers are present when you have the thoughts.

UNDERSTANDING THAT THOUGHTS CHANGE

Like Skyler, you may think you're the only one who thinks about suicide. And you may think you'll always think about suicide. Both these conclusions are understandable. But neither is really true. Consider a silly thought you had recently, like *I wonder what cats dream about?* This thought wasn't present in your mind before you thought it and it won't always be present in the future— at some point, you'll stop thinking it (unless you're a cat-dream whisperer; but even if you are, you'll still probably stop thinking it at some point). Thoughts come into and pass out of your mind all the time, which means your thoughts change. Of course, some thoughts are stickier than others, meaning they tend to get stuck in your mind. Sometimes suicidal thoughts can be sticky; you just can't seem to get them out of your head! But if you monitor your thoughts closely, you'll find that the sticky thoughts aren't *always* present. Even sticky thoughts change! As you complete the activities in this book, you'll become more skilled at recognizing and enjoying the times when suicidal thoughts aren't present, as well as using coping strategies to make your suicidal thoughts less sticky so they can slip out of your mind (perhaps with you giving them a nudge!).

To illustrate this point, let's return to Skyler. Recall that Skyler felt like an outcast and argued with her caregivers daily. Skyler starting thinking that life was too painful to go on and that dying would be a big relief. But Skyler hadn't always thought that way. Skyler had had some really fun moments in the last year. Even though she finds her parents annoying and overbearing at times, she felt special, loved, and happy when they attended her marching band performance and told her she was amazing. She also had fun hanging out and goofing around with her friends during band camp in the summer. In those fun moments, Skyler wasn't thinking about dying. So her thoughts about suicide had come and gone over the past year. What's more, her thoughts even changed from day to day. For example, when she plays with the band, Skyler is focused on the music (and having fun!) and not on ending her life. Thoughts about ending her life tend to happen most commonly when she's alone in her room at night or after she has a fight with her parents. By developing awareness of when, where, and under what circumstances her thoughts of suicide happened (and did not happen), Skyler was able to start taking actions to gain control over her suicidal thoughts.

To further illustrate the point that thoughts change, try the following exercise. Reflect on these questions, or better yet, write your answers in your journal so you can come back to them later.

- What was your favorite television show five years ago? Is it the same now?

- What was something you believed in the past that you no longer believe?

- Have you always had suicidal thoughts? Name a time in the past when you didn't.

- Have you ever had a crush on someone, but your thoughts and feelings about that person changed over time?

What did you learn from this exercise? Have your thoughts and feelings all stayed the same or have they changed over time? Our hunch is that your thoughts and feelings have changed—they come, they go, sometimes they come back, and sometimes they never come back. The same is true with thoughts about suicide. Sometimes you think about suicide, especially when you experience the reasons listed earlier in this chapter, but you won't always think about suicide.

Research shows that teenagers are more likely to experience suicidal thoughts than any other age group. Research also shows that most teenagers who experience suicidal thoughts no longer experience those thoughts when they are adults. Remember that about one in five high school students thinks about suicide every year (Ivey-Stephenson et al., 2020). Only about one in twenty adults thinks about suicide every year (Substance Abuse and Mental Health Services Administration, 2020). What explains this huge difference? Thoughts change over time! Specifically, suicidal thoughts become less common as people enter adulthood. It usually gets better over time.

There are a few reasons why this happens. One, there is less rapid change and stress in adulthood than in the teen years. Of course, stressful experiences still occur in adulthood, but our relationships with people and our routines tend to become more stable as adults, and more stability usually means less stress. Two, going through change and stress as a teen helps you develop skills to manage stress better, so that when you do experience stress as an adult, you're better equipped to cope with it. Three, our brains reach maturity in adulthood—specifically, the parts of our brains that are involved in regulating our emotional experiences continue developing up through about age twenty-five, so the intensity of our negative emotional experiences tends to decrease in adulthood and our ability to regulate those experiences tends to increase. The result typically is a smoother journey in adulthood. That's something you can look forward to.

In the meantime, if you can learn to understand your patterns of thinking, to evaluate whether your thoughts are accurate to a situation and what you can do to help yourself when difficult thoughts arise, you can learn to deal with the suicidal thoughts you experience. This book will help you learn to do that.

MOVING FORWARD

In this chapter, you have identified where you are at in your journey and what gear you need, including this book and a journal. This book can be helpful no matter where you're at, but there may be times when you need extra help. That's why it's important to understand when you need extra help and how to find it. As you continue on your journey, remember that you're not alone—many other people are on similar journeys and can relate to your thoughts and experiences. Also, remember that thoughts change—if you're experiencing suicidal thoughts now, don't give up, because they'll change! This book is based on a lot of research and lived experience showing that teens can learn skills to change their suicidal thoughts and live happier lives.

In the rest of this book, we'll cover ways to help you deal with the suicidal thoughts you experience. You'll learn how to identify and manage your feelings and thoughts, and the things that stress you out. You'll also learn to build friendships and social support so you always have someone to turn to when you need help. And you'll explore your purpose—the things you might want to do in your life, things that will help you feel excitement and joy for the future again, even if that might feel kind of impossible now.

We also need to make sure you stay safe here and now. So the next chapter will be about making yourself a safety plan—one you can use when things get hard, your negative thoughts get loud, and you feel overwhelmed, like you might hurt yourself.

CHAPTER 2

Starting Out with Safety Planning

On your journey through life, it is important to be prepared for the road ahead. For a hike, you might need a map, a water bottle, and a fully charged phone. As a teen struggling with suicidal thoughts, you can also prepare for the road ahead by taking steps to stay safe. This chapter is all about coping with thoughts of suicide now and planning for your safety. Later chapters will focus on new skills and strategies for reducing thoughts of suicide and building a life worth living.

The information and activities in this chapter are pretty intense. This chapter is in the front of the book because your safety is important. But that also means not just dipping your toes in to test the water—it's time to dive right in.

STAYING SAFE IN A CRISIS

Imagine you get news that a hurricane is heading your way. The weatherperson and city officials advise everyone to take a few basic steps: board up your windows, stock up on clean water and food, and make sure you have a flashlight and first aid kit. Would you take their advice and follow these steps? They certainly seem like a lot of extra work! You might not need the extra food or water, the power might not go out, the hurricane might shift its path and miss you entirely. So why bother with these precautions? These steps are designed to keep you safe in case the storm *does* hit and puts your life in danger.

In the same way, this section is about making sure your home is a safe place for you in a suicide-related emergency. If your suicidal thoughts become too intense to control, making your home a safe place can help protect you. The idea is to place as many barriers as possible between you and suicidal behavior. For example, if your suicidal thoughts—or your mental image of what suicide looks like—include overdosing on pills or medications, then it's a good idea to remove extra pills from your home.

Find the Danger Points

To make your home a safe place, start by identifying all potentially dangerous items that need to be safely secured (Suicide Prevention Resource Center, 2021). There are two items that should *always* be safely stored if you have them in your home. The first is firearms. Just over half of all suicide deaths in the United States involve firearms. Even if your suicidal thoughts do not include using a firearm, having access to a gun when you are thinking about suicide is extremely dangerous. So it's essential to remove or secure any firearms in your home.

The second item you should always secure is medications. Medication overdose is the most common way that young people attempt suicide. Most homes have at least a few medications, whether prescribed by a doctor or purchased over the counter. Locking up these medications is another important step toward making your home a safer place. With your caregiver's help, you can lock up medications and pills in a safe or cash box, with your caregiver taking charge of the key so only they have access. That way, if you become upset and think about taking a bunch of pills, you won't be able to. It may not seem like much, but placing a barrier between you and suicidal behavior can mean the difference between life and death.

You should also consider securing any other items that you have had thoughts about using to harm yourself. When you think about suicide, what do you picture in your mind? If your mental image of suicide includes any specific items, be sure to secure those as well. These may include sharp objects, such as knives or razor blades; poisons or chemicals, such as bleach or cleaning products; or belts, ropes, or neckties. The Letter to Caregivers provided here has detailed information on how to store each of these items safely.

Get Help: Action Steps for Caregivers

Now that you know *what* to store, the next step is to get those items stored safely. For this, you'll likely need some help from a caregiver. Having a caregiver involved is an important part of making your home safe, and ultimately it is up to your caregiver to remove and lock up or secure these items. But talking with a caregiver about suicide can be uncomfortable, intimidating, even scary. To try to make this easier and help explain to your caregiver how they can help, we've included a sample letter you can share with them. The letter explains the purpose of this step of your safety plan and has some helpful tips for storing items safely. Be sure to also share your list with them, so that they know which objects they need to lock up or remove!

Once you've shared the letter with your caregivers, be sure to thank them for their help. Then continue building your safety plan in the next section.

Dear Caregivers,

Your child is taking important steps to help keep themself safe and manage their suicidal thoughts. Now they need your help. One of the most important steps you can take is to help keep your child safe at home by removing or locking up items that could be used for suicide. This is called *means safety,* and it's proven effective in preventing suicide. Evidence shows that although suicidal urges can be intense, they are often brief. That's why the goal of means safety is to put as many steps as possible between your child and the means to attempt suicide—delaying even just a few minutes could save their life.

A few things to know: First, your child should have identified which things need to be secured. This should include any firearms, medications, and any other items your child has selected. It is up to you to make sure these items are secured.

To secure firearms: The best option is, if possible, to remove any firearms from your home entirely. If they aren't in your home, they can't be used to harm your child. If that's not possible, then make sure all firearms are locked in a safe or gun locker, with ammunition stored separately in another safe or lockbox. Remove the firing pin or add an extra trigger lock, and be sure to check the chamber for an additional round.

Medications: Almost every household has at least a few medications. Since some over-the-counter medications can be dangerous, especially in large quantities or when combined with other medications, it is important that *all* medications be locked up, whether over-the-counter or prescription—even common pain relievers or cold medicine. A safe or lock box is a good choice. If someone in your household needs to take medications daily, a one- or two-day supply of needed medications can be left available, unless those medications are particularly dangerous.

Knives: Knives, razors, scissors, and other sharp tools can be stored in a lockbox or safe. Knife drawers can also be secured with a simple latch and standard combination lock.

Household chemicals: Household cleaning products such as bleach, toilet cleaner, laundry detergent, or other caustic chemicals can be stored in a locked cabinet or disposed of entirely (there are safer, equally effective options). Inventory all the different chemicals you have in your home—check closets, garages, and under sinks to make sure you have found everything.

Belts, ropes, and neckties: These items can be locked up in a cabinet or safe. While it can be difficult to lock away all such everyday items, the obvious targets can be removed, making it more difficult to die by suicide in this manner. Remember, the goal is to put a barrier between your child and suicidal behavior, so even removing common objects can be helpful. And be certain to consider all family members' belts and neckties, not just your own.

A few important details:

1. Make sure your child does not have access to any keys, combinations, or passcodes to open any cabinets, locks, or safes. Use a unique passcode that only you know, and don't share it with your child. Keys should be kept safely with a family member, not lying around and not "hidden" where they might be easily found.

2. Hiding is *not* the same as securing. Hiding objects in a closet or cabinet is not enough—the purpose of this step is to ensure that your child can't access these items during a crisis. Hiding places can be discovered; locks are harder to break.

Many people are concerned that locking up common household items might be inconvenient—and it can be. Remember that this situation is temporary. With time and appropriate care from a mental health professional, suicidal thoughts and urges are treatable. Eventually, once concerns about suicide are sufficiently reduced, these objects can be returned or unlocked. But your child's safety is a priority, and accepting some inconvenience now can potentially save their life. Thank you for taking steps to help keep your child safe.

Set yourself a reminder to check in with your caregiver in a couple of days. Make sure they follow through on securing these items. Just like you, adults need a reminder sometimes! Set a notification in your phone or write a note in your planner—and be sure to remind this person to secure the items you have identified.

HAVING A PLAN HELPS

The next step for taking control of your thoughts of suicide is to make a plan for what to do when thoughts of suicide happen. That way, you will know how to keep yourself safe. In later chapters, you will take additional steps as you learn how to challenge and change your suicidal thoughts. You will also learn new skills and strategies to prevent them from happening and to build a life with purpose. But first, it's important to have a plan for coping with thoughts of suicide (Stanley & Brown, 2012; Hill et al., 2020).

The next few sections will help you build your own plan. The steps are arranged in order, from least intense to most intense. That way you can start small and try to handle your thoughts on your own. But if coping on your own is not enough—and sometimes it may not be—you will know what to try next. Your plan will include a range of activities, like distracting yourself or using coping skills, spending time with other people, and asking others for help when you need support.

Most important, your plan will build on your strengths. Different strategies work for different people. Your plan should be designed to work for you, not for someone else. It will draw on your interests and skills and the relationships you already have to give you the support you need.

Step 1: Get Engaged!

In the first step, you'll rely on your existing coping skills. We all have things that we do to cope with challenging or stressful times. And we all do things to distract ourselves from what is bothering us, to enjoy ourselves when we are down, or to just take a break from a stressful day. This section will help you identify your skills and then select the healthiest and most useful ones. In essence, in this first step you'll try to distract yourself from your suicidal thoughts or from the problem or situation you are struggling with. Sometimes, through your keeping your mind busy, the suicidal thoughts get pushed aside. To be clear, this step is *not* simply "trying to not think about suicide." Instead, you should be actively engaged in something you really enjoy. You want to try and create a positive experience that can improve your mood, while also putting some distance between you and the events that led you to think about suicide. Sometimes a little bit of space can help make problems seem less overwhelming. This step also starts to put you back in control, letting you handle things on your own terms.

The goal of this step is to do something on your own that is active and distracting, something that will keep you focused and interested. Try to think of activities that you can lose yourself in—things you can do for a long time while completely ignoring everything else. Those are great activities, because they help you focus on the moment and not on your suicidal thoughts, problems, or worries.

Create a Menu of Options

Imagine that someone in your town opens a brand-new restaurant. You've never been there before, but the place looks nice, so you decide to give it a try. You go in, get a table, and the waiter hands you the menu. When you open it up, you discover that the restaurant serves just one dish. That's not a menu! There aren't any options! It might be fine to have the dish once, but even if it's your favorite meal, you probably wouldn't want to eat there every day. A good menu should have enough options to be satisfying—different things to try on different days. Variety keeps things interesting.

In the same way, your safety plan should have several different activities, so you have a menu of options to choose from. One day you might want to read a book; another day you might be more interested in sketching in your notepad or taking your dog for a walk. If you don't have enough options, your safety plan will get boring too quickly.

Grab your notebook and start by making a list. First, think about the things you do when you want to have fun. List a few things that make you feel good or make you smile. Next, think of things you do to relax or unwind when you've had a difficult day. What makes you feel calm or puts you at ease? Add those to the list. Don't worry if you can't name many things—this book will help you build more skills in the coming sections.

Now list anything that you do to feel better when you are down, sad, or disappointed. What do you do to cope with difficult times in your life? Add these to your list.

Your list might look something like this:

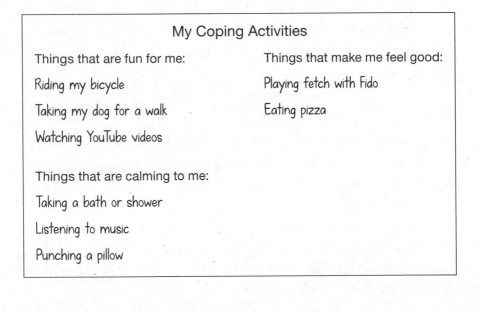

My Coping Activities

Things that are fun for me:

Riding my bicycle

Taking my dog for a walk

Watching YouTube videos

Things that are calming to me:

Taking a bath or shower

Listening to music

Punching a pillow

Things that make me feel good:

Playing fetch with Fido

Eating pizza

If it's hard to think of things, take a look at the following suggestions for well-known mood lifters. Maybe you already do some of these things. If so, add them to your list!

Get Engaged! Activities You Can Do On Your Own	
Take your dog for a walk.	Put together a jigsaw puzzle.
Play with your cat.	Write a story.
Go for a run or jog.	Paint a picture.
Exercise.	Wash the car.
Draw a picture.	Clean up your room.
Sketch in your notebook.	Play video games.
Make a YouTube video.	Play a board or card game.
Start an art project.	Read a good book.
Bake cookies.	Learn a language.
Take a shower or bath.	Learn to play an instrument.
Take a walk.	Build something.
Learn some photography skills.	Play your favorite sport.
Dance!	Watch funny videos.
Ride your bicycle.	Create a comic book.
Take a bubble bath.	Meditate.
Practice your free throws.	Learn something new.

The more helpful skills and activities you can find, the better! Now that you have a list of possible activities, select a few for your safety plan. Be certain to select things you can do at home, at school, or wherever else you spend a lot of time. To keep things fresh and interesting, try to come up with four or five activities, but make sure you have *at least* three.

My "Get Engaged" Activity Menu

Play video games—soccer or basketball.

Take the dog for a walk at the park.

Sketch in my notepad.

Read Harry Potter books in my room.

Practice the guitar.

Review Your Menu—and Make Improvements

Now take a few minutes to review the activities you listed. Complete each of the following activity checks to improve your chances of success!

Activity Check #1: Are all of the activities on your list things you can do for *at least* fifteen or twenty minutes? If not, add a few more activities or replace some of the shorter ones.

Activity Check #2: Did you list something you can do at home? At school? If you spend time at more than one home, do you have activities you can do wherever you live? If not, try to add at least one thing for every place you spend a lot of your time.

Activity Check #3: Do any of your activities need supplies? For example, if you listed "Bake cookies," do you have all the ingredients you need? If you wrote "Sketch in my notepad," do you need colored pencils or markers? If you don't have the supplies needed, can you ask your caregiver for them? Or would it be better to select a different activity? Make changes to your list if needed.

Activity Check #4: Do you need permission to do any of your activities? For example, if you listed "Play video games" but your caregiver has a rule about not playing video games on a school night, that could be a problem. If you need permission for your activities, have a conversation with your caregiver ahead of time, or list some other activity.

Activity Check #5: When you are upset, it can help to have specific steps to follow. The more specific your activities are, the easier it will be to use your safety plan. Take a moment to make each of your activities as specific as you can. For example, instead of "Play with my dog" you could write "Take Fido for a walk around the block" or "Teach Peaches how to play fetch." Instead of "Read a good book" you could write, "Read a Harry Potter book on the living room couch."

Activity Check #6: Is there anything on your list that could cause harm to you or someone else? Some things we do to help us to feel better in the short term can make us feel worse in the long term. We call these *instant relief traps*. Like eating an entire tray of cookies when you are really hungry, instant relief traps might help you feel better now but cause trouble down the road. For that reason, they are best avoided altogether. Don't set yourself up for more challenges later on! For example, some people turn to alcohol or drugs when they are feeling down. Though this may make them feel better for a little while, using alcohol or drugs to cope with tough situations has negative long-term effects: you could get into legal trouble; you could become addicted or get in trouble at home or at school. Instant relief traps like cutting yourself, overeating, or hitting or breaking things can all lead to bigger problems. These traps differ from activities like playing a game or walking your dog, which aren't likely to lead to long-term problems. If you have anything on your list that might be an instant relief trap, kick it to the curb! Look through your list and cross out any likely traps.

There are plenty of better coping activities to choose from—you just have to find the right ones!

Now review your menu, using the Activity Checks, and make changes if needed.

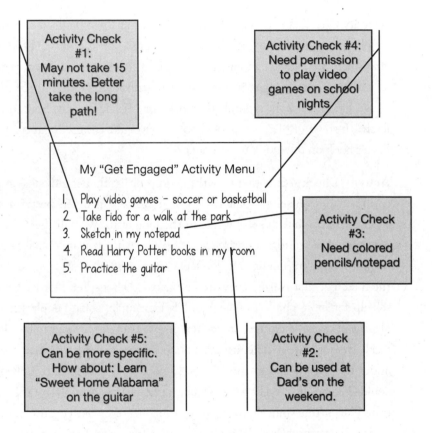

Take some time to try out all your activities over the next week. Were they distracting? Did you have fun? If an activity helped you to stay busy and kept you engaged, then it's good to keep on your list. If one wasn't very distracting or didn't take long enough, or if you had trouble completing the activity, then make changes. No list is perfect on the first try! So try things out, see how they work, and make changes as you go.

Step 2: Be Social!

In the previous section, you selected activities to try to cope with or distract yourself from your suicidal thoughts. Trying to handle things on your own is a good starting point. If you start to think about suicide, you should look at your list of activities and pick one to try. Your chosen activity is intended to distract you enough that your suicidal thoughts have passed by the time you finish.

Sometimes thoughts of suicide are more persistent. If doing something on your own isn't enough to get your thoughts under control, it's time to involve other people. It's time for the next step in your plan: Being social.

The Power of Social Connections .

Humans are social. We like to be around other people. Whether we talk about the news, tell stories, or discuss our favorite television shows, engaging with other people tends to raise our spirits and improve our mood. So although trying to manage suicidal thoughts on your own is a good start, the next step is to be social and spend some time with at least one other person.

When you have thoughts about suicide, you might feel like being alone. Being alone isn't always a bad thing. If you need time and space to focus, like for doing homework or planning a project, being alone can be helpful. If you are upset or angry, being alone can help you calm down, think things through, and avoid people who might be annoying you. But when you have thoughts of suicide, being alone with your thoughts can be more harmful than helpful. Even though you might think being alone will make you feel better, you might end up going over and over your thoughts of suicide. Psychologists call this *ruminating.* Ruminating on your thoughts of suicide—or the things that led you to think about suicide in the first place—can actually leave you feeling even more lonely, rejected, or hopeless.

Instead of isolating yourself, try to actively seek out other people. This could be a friend, family member, neighbor, or anyone you like to talk to and spend time with. You can visit this person, call them, or video chat—anything that gives you a live, in-the-moment connection. You don't even have to talk about what is bothering you! Another option is to go somewhere public, like a local basketball court, library, café, or school sports event, where you can be around other people.

Who can you talk to or spend some time with? Grab a notebook and start by making a list of people you like to spend time with, enjoy talking to, or would like to hang out with more often. These could be family members, like a sibling, parent, step-parent, cousin, aunt or uncle, niece or nephew, or grand-parent. They might be friends, teammates, classmates, or coworkers. They could also be a trusted neighbor or teacher. Try to come up with three to five people you can comfortably talk to or spend time with.

Where can you go to be around people? What sorts of places do you have available to you? Add these places to your list. This might be a little more difficult. Many kids your age don't have a driver's license and may not be able to go many places. It may not be safe to be out at night, or you might need a caregiver's permission. (As of this writing, there have been a couple years of changing pandemic restrictions, and the future is unpredictable; just keep the current situation in mind.) Think of any places that you *can* go, and add those to your list. This might include a friend's or neighbor's home or a local park, café, library, or community center.

> ## My List of People I Can Talk to and Places I Can Go!
>
> "Be Social:" People I Can Talk To
>
> My cousin Sam
>
> Mom
>
> Alysha from the basketball team
>
> My friend Tommy
>
> "Be Social:" Places I Can Go
>
> Head to the basketball court for a pick-up game.
>
> Walk to Starbucks and get a latte.

Friends, peers, and classmates are all good choices for being social. If you're having trouble thinking of people to add to your list, try asking around. Ask someone you trust who they talk to when they need to be around people. They may give you some ideas about who to include. Remember, this step is just spending time with someone; you don't have to talk to them about personal things or the way you are feeling (that comes next).

Step 3: Asking for Help

Imagine this for a moment: You get into an argument with your caregivers. You are upset and angry and start to have thoughts of suicide. Maybe you think your caregiver would be happier without you. Maybe you think suicide is the best way to solve a problem you're having. But you've been working through this book, and you recognize that you need to use your safety plan. So you look at your activities and decide to try taking your dog for a walk. After walking around the park for a bit, you aren't feeling any better. You are *still* thinking about suicide. So you move on to the next step of your plan and call your best friend. The two of you chat for a while about school and sports. But even after talking to your best friend, you still aren't feeling better, and your thoughts of suicide are still there. It's time to take a new approach.

When problems seem overwhelming or just too big to handle on our own, we need to rely on others to assist us. You've tried to distract yourself from the problem so that time can help make things easier to handle. You've focused on staying engaged with other things. But you haven't been actively tackling the reason for your thoughts of suicide. Now it's time to address the issue head on—and that means getting help.

Every hero needs a good partner—someone to rely on when things get tough, to offer support or advice, to be a friend. Sherlock Holmes has Dr. Watson, Wonder Woman has Wonder Girl, T'Challa (Black Panther) has Shuri and Okoye, and Han Solo has Chewbacca! The point is, even geniuses, superheroes, and spaceship pilots need help sometimes. Think of this step as finding your partner—the person who can help you out when it feels like the world is too much to handle on your own.

So this step of your safety plan is reaching out for help or support. You're going to identify and connect with some safe adults you can turn to for help—people who can listen to your situation, help you find a solution, and provide some hope that things *will* get better.

What Makes a Good Helper?

Selecting the right people for this step of your safety plan is important. Now you're seeking someone who will sit and listen to what's going on in your life, offer solutions, and try to help with what's troubling you. Those are probably different people from those you listed in the previous step to distract you from your suicidal thoughts—the friends, siblings, and others your age you could to talk to about common interests or enjoy activities with, without going into deeper or painful areas.

So what are you looking for in a good helper? Start with someone who is a good listener! If you're going to share your problems, you want to make sure the person is willing to listen and hear you out. You'll also want someone who can step in and help, who can offer solutions and help you bring about real changes in your life. You might want someone with more experience than you, someone who has been around a bit and might have dealt with similar problems themself.

In short, a good helper is likely to be an adult. Remember, you aren't looking for someone to distract you or make you feel better. You are looking for someone to help you manage the problems life is throwing at you. Sometimes when problems seem too big to handle, it takes an adult to help. Adults have more experience and can offer solutions and supports you might not have thought of on your own.

Who are the adults in your life who might be able to help? Caregivers or family members can be a great source of help and assistance. But some people aren't comfortable talking to their family—this is very common. There are other adults you can reach out to for assistance. The important thing is to select people you feel comfortable talking to—people you think will be a good support when you need them.

Start by listing some possibilities in your notebook. Who are the adults you know well enough to talk with? Don't rule anyone out just yet—start by making a list of *all* the adults you know. It may surprise you to find that many people are willing to listen and help when you ask them to.

We have lots of people in our lives! We just might not realize it. Here are some of the adults you might have in your life, to consider as you brainstorm and make your list:

Caregivers/Parents	Teachers
Coach or team leader	Uncles
Step-parents	A school counselor
Faith leaders	Older siblings
Grandparents	Parents of your friends
Neighbors	Adult cousins
Aunts	Friends of your parents

Now begin to narrow your list down, selecting three or four adults you are most comfortable talking to. Choose adults you can talk to in different settings: at school, at home, or on the weekends.

Try to find a few helpful adults that you can talk to, and make a list like this one.

My Helpful Adults

Grandma Maria

Uncle Emilio

Coach Johnson

Mr. Green, my geometry teacher

An Informed Partner Is a Helpful Partner

You'll find that most adults are happy to listen and help. But if they don't already know that you've chosen them, they might not pick up the phone or respond to your text message right away. So it's helpful to have a short conversation with each of the adults you've selected.

This might be a scary conversation to have! It can help to have an idea of what you want to say and even practice it by yourself. It might sound something like this: "Hey Coach, have a minute? I'm trying to do a better job of managing my stress and keeping myself healthy. Sometimes, when my problems get overwhelming, I need someone to talk to who can help me out. You know me pretty well, and I'm comfortable talking to you. Would it be okay if I talked with you when I need some help?"

Step 4: Professional Helpers

If none of the previous steps have helped you get your suicidal thoughts under control, then it is time to contact a professional. If at *any* time your suicidal thoughts or urges feel out of control, or if you are worried you will act on them and harm yourself, you should seek help from a professional right away. The previous steps can help you manage your suicidal thoughts, and it is important that you try them, but if you *know* you need professional help, you should skip straight to this step.

There are three main ways to seek professional help in a crisis:

Choice 1: If you have a therapist or counselor, give that person a telephone call. First ask your therapist in a scheduled session whether they are available for calls or can offer an alternative.

Choice 2: Try contacting a crisis hotline. There are several different suicide prevention–focused hotlines, available twenty-four hours a day, seven days a week, staffed by trained professionals who can help. The National Suicide Prevention Lifeline is one; their phone number is 988. Calling is free, and counselors are available any time, day or night. If you prefer not to talk on the phone, contact the Crisis Text Line by texting the message "home" to the number 741741. They will link you with a trained support person who will reply via text message. Again, you can text any time, day or night. The Trevor Project, designed specifically to help and support LGBTQ people, also has a phone hotline (1-866-488-7386) and text hotline (text "START" to 678678). (See the Resources section for more information.)

Choice 3: In any emergency, call 911 or go to your local hospital emergency room.

Take some time to check out all of these professional help resources. Visit the National Suicide Prevention Lifeline or Crisis Text Line websites. Head over to the Trevor Project website or look up the American Foundation for Suicide Prevention. There are lots of resources online that may be helpful. (See the Resources section for a complete list.)

Putting It All Together: Build Your Safety Plan

Now that you have all the pieces to your safety plan, it's time to put them together! Remember, your safety plan is designed to work as a step-by-step guide. You start with coping on your own, then being social, then asking for help informally, and finally, seeking professional help. At each step, you have a little menu of activities to choose from or people to talk to.

When you put it all together, your safety plan should look something like this:

My Safety Plan

Step 1. Get Engaged! Ways I can cope on my own.

Pick an activity:

- Play video games—soccer or basketball.
- Take Fido for a walk at the park.
- Sketch in my notepad.
- Read Harry Potter books in my room.
- Practice the guitar.

Step 2. Be Social!

People I can talk to. (Talk to one of them.)

- My cousin Sam
- Mom
- Alysha from the basketball team
- My friend Tommy

Places I can go. (Go somewhere public.)

- Head to the basketball court for a pick-up game.
- Walk to Starbucks and get a latte.

Step 3. My Helpful Adults (Talk to one of them.)

- Grandma Maria
- Uncle Emilio
- Coach Johnson
- Mr. Green, my geometry teacher

Step 4. Call a Professional (Contact one of these in an emergency.)

- Call the National Suicide Prevention Lifeline: 988.
- Text "home" to the Crisis Text Line: 741741.
- Call 911 or go to an emergency room.

Now your safety plan is ready to go. Of course, your safety plan works only if you use it. So make sure you have access to your plan whenever and wherever you need it. That way, no matter where you are when suicidal thoughts arise, you have your plan available to support you.

How will you make sure your safety plan is available? You could take a photo and store it in your phone. Or put a copy in your wallet, purse, or backpack. There are apps for this, too. You might tape a copy to your bedroom mirror or keep a copy on your kitchen fridge. Take whatever steps you need to so your safety plan is always waiting when you need it.

Don't Give Up

Having a safety plan is a great start! The first few times you use it, you may find that you need most or all of the steps to get your suicidal thoughts under control. That's okay. That's what the plan is there for. With time and practice, you'll likely find that you need fewer steps to get control of your suicidal thoughts and start to feel better.

Safety plans are almost never perfect on the first try. Maybe you'll use your safety plan and find that one of the activities isn't helping. Or maybe one of your social contacts doesn't pick up the phone or respond to your messages. If that happens, change, edit, or remake your safety plan as often as needed until it works well for you. Your safety plan is a work in progress. Pay attention to how well your safety plan is working, and be sure to make changes when you need to.

MOVING FORWARD

Now that you've got your safety plan, let's move on to the next stage of your journey! In the next section, you will learn about different feelings and how to recognize what you are feeling. You'll also learn new skills for managing your emotions when they start to get out of control.

CHAPTER 3

Identifying and Managing Feelings

In the first two chapters, you learned to identify when you need extra help on your journey and made yourself a plan to stay safe when times get tough. You're now ready to take the next step—learning how to identify and manage the feelings you experience.

Feelings, or emotions, can put you on a roller coaster, from peaks of joy to valleys of despair and every point in between. Why do we experience emotions? Scientists generally agree that the purpose of emotions is to prepare us to deal with something without having to think about it too much. That means emotions happen without your choosing to experience them. But the fact that you experience feelings without consciously choosing to doesn't mean you can't manage them effectively.

Throughout this chapter, we'll talk about *managing* your feelings—not controlling them. This choice of words is intentional. As we'll discuss later, it's really difficult, if not impossible, to control your in-the-moment feelings. In fact, trying to control your feelings usually backfires, leaving you frustrated, feeling helpless and maybe even hopeless about feeling better. So instead of trying to control your feelings, you'll learn how to manage them.

Managing your feelings is like being a coach. Think about what a coach does: organizing a team, identifying its strengths and weaknesses. An effective coach can't control the team, nor can she make the team's weaknesses completely disappear. Instead, she develops strategies to get the most out of the team's strengths and overcome its weaknesses, which can lead to greater success. You can apply the same idea to your feelings. You can't control what you feel, nor can you make your negative feelings completely disappear, but you can develop strategies to manage your feelings so you can act in ways consistent with your values and goals, and ultimately enjoy success in life.

So how do you become an effective coach, or manager, of your feelings? An important first step is learning to read your signs.

READING YOUR SIGNS

On any journey, it's important to pay attention to signs, because they tell you where you are and how to get where you want to go. Emotions, or feelings, are internal signs that tell you where you're at and what direction you should take. For example, if you feel angry, that's a sign telling you that something's not right and you might need to take an off-ramp to defuse the situation before something bad happens. If you feel happy, that's a sign telling you something is right and you should stay on the same path and keep doing what you're doing to savor the moment!

The idea that emotions are signs is pretty obvious, right? But it can be hard to accurately read and understand signs. If you have your driver's license, think about all the road signs you had to learn before you took the driving test. Some of them don't make sense at first glance; the only way to understand them is to study the driver's guide. The same is true when it comes to reading and understanding your emotions accurately. In the rest of this chapter, you'll learn how to get in touch with your emotions; then you'll learn tips for managing them, especially your unpleasant emotions. For ease of communication, we'll use the terms *emotions* and *feelings* interchangeably in this chapter.

IDENTIFYING, LABELING, AND RATING YOUR FEELINGS

What is emotion? We all experience emotions and know more or less what they are, but they're hard to define. And sometimes it's hard to recognize and label our emotions. Have you ever had a general "bad" feeling, but you weren't able to put your finger on exactly what it was? You're not alone—many people have that experience! Learning how to tell the differences between your emotions and how to accurately label them is an important step toward learning how to manage them (Brent, Poling, & Goldstein, 2011). Suicidal thoughts often occur when people experience intense negative emotions like sadness and anger. They can also occur when people *don't* experience positive emotions like happiness. By learning how to manage your emotions, you'll be better equipped to shut down suicidal thoughts when they appear and, in many cases, prevent them from appearing in the first place.

So let's get clear on emotions. Scientists generally agree that there are five *basic* emotions: joy, fear, anger, sadness, and disgust. Some scientists also include surprise and contempt as basic emotions. All the different feelings you experience arise from these five to seven basic emotions and thoughts related to these basic emotions.

The quickest way to become skilled at identifying and labeling feelings is by expanding your feelings vocabulary—the words you use to describe feelings. With a larger feelings vocabulary, you'll be able to move beyond describing your feeling in general terms like "good" or "bad" to using precise terms that pinpoint exactly what you're experiencing.

Look at the following list of feelings. See if you can come up with another word for each feeling and write it down in your journal. If you can come up with two or three words for a feeling, even better! Generating names of different feelings is a good way to build your feelings vocabulary. If you find it hard to come up with other words for a feeling, use a thesaurus (you can find one online).

Affectionate	Determined	Hopeful	Proud
Amazed	Disappointed	Hopeless	Relaxed
Angry	Discouraged	Hurt	Resentful
Afraid	Disgusted	Impatient	Sad
Annoyed	Distracted	Impulsive	Silly
Anxious	Embarrassed	Inspired	Satisfied
Ashamed	Empty	Interested	Serene
Attentive	Energetic	Irate	Serious
Bored	Enthusiastic	Irritable	Sorry
Brave	Enraged	Jealous	Stubborn
Calm	Excited	Joyful	Surprised
Cautious	Frustrated	Lonely	Sympathetic
Cheerful	Funny	Loving	Thankful
Compassionate	Gloomy	Misunderstood	Timid
Confident	Grouchy	Nervous	Tired
Concerned	Guilty	Neutral	Unsure
Confused	Happy	Numb	Withdrawn
Content	Hateful	Optimistic	Worried
Curious	Heartbroken	Overwhelmed	
Depressed	Helpless	Playful	

Now try to remember a time when you felt each of the feelings that these words indicate. That's a lot of words, so it's okay to pick just a handful of them. Make sure you pick a mix of positive and negative words. Reflect on what you felt in your body and what thoughts were going through your mind when you had each feeling. For example, for the word *anxious* you might have butterflies in your stomach, sweaty palms, and muscle tension in your neck, and thoughts of *What will people think of me? Can they see me sweating?* and *What if I mess up in front of everyone?* For each word you pick, write notes in your journal describing what you felt and what you were doing and thinking. Reflecting on and writing down your feelings, thoughts, and experiences will help you become more aware of your feelings and more skilled at recognizing and labeling them.

Another way to get better at identifying feelings is to watch videos, shows, or movies and see if you can tell what emotion the character is feeling. Pick a character in one of your favorite shows, focus on a specific scene, and then try to use as many different words as you can to label what they are feeling. You can refer back to the list of words on the preceding page if it helps you label more precisely what the character is feeling. Then pick a different character and do it again! The more you practice, the more you'll build your awareness of emotions and feelings that people experience.

As you practice, you'll find that sometimes it's really easy to identify and label what characters are feeling based on their actions and contexts. For example, if a character is crying (action) after their dog died (context), it's obvious they're sad, heartbroken, or devastated. If a character is yelling at another driver (action) after getting cut off in traffic (context), it's clear they're angry, irate, furious, or enraged. Other times, though, it's hard to identify and label emotions. Sometimes people feel neutral—there is no big emotion present. For example, a character who is walking down the street, or reading a book, or sitting in class might feel neutral. Or they might not, depending on what thoughts they are experiencing. In these examples, their actions and contexts don't make it clear exactly what they're feeling. Regardless, try your best to identify what characters are feeling based on their actions and the contexts.

Once you have practiced identifying feelings in several characters, try it on yourself! Set your alarm at various times during the day, and when the alarm sounds, use one of the feeling words from the list to describe yourself. Keep in mind that you won't always experience a big emotion; sometimes you may feel neutral. That's okay—write that down in your journal too. Go ahead and try doing this now; we will come back to it later in this chapter. Practicing this regularly will make you more attuned to your feelings and build your awareness of emotions. It also will make it easier for you to recognize when your feelings change. Again, building this awareness is a key first step to understanding and managing your feelings.

In addition to accurately identifying *what* you feel, the *intensity* of your feelings can tell you when and how to use strategies to manage your emotions. Feelings are not an all-or-nothing experience. We experience feelings on a range of intensity. If you feel inspired, you could be just a little inspired, very inspired, or super over-the-top inspired! The same is true for other feelings. If you're feeling an emotion like anger very intensely, it might be a sign to use some calming techniques. Or, if you're feeling super blah, it might be a sign to use a strategy for boosting positive emotions. We'll talk more about these strategies later in the chapter. For now, let's focus on identifying how intense your feelings are.

To measure the intensity of your feelings, you can use a feelings thermometer like the one shown on the following page. A rating of 1 means you barely have the feeling at all; 2 means the feeling is present but weak; 3 means it's medium—not weak but not strong; 4 means the feeling is strong; 5 means the feeling is very intense.

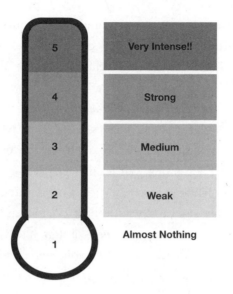

To illustrate how the feelings thermometer works, consider Juan. Juan gets anxious when he speaks to other people, especially people he doesn't know well. He prefers to hang out with his small circle of friends and family; that's where he feels comfortable. He feels nervous when he has to talk to people outside his circle, but he manages it okay. He gets super nervous and even sick to his stomach when he has to give a presentation at school. He usually takes a zero for the assignment instead of giving presentations. Here are examples of Juan's anxiety ratings around other people.

Talking on the phone to someone he knows well	1: A tiny bit anxious, almost nothing
Ordering food at a restaurant	2: A little anxious
Making small talk with teens he doesn't know well	3: Pretty anxious
Asking adults for something he needs	4: Very anxious
Giving a class presentation in school	5: Extremely anxious!

Think about the intensity of your feelings. As you practice identifying and labeling them, start rating their intensity on the thermometer. If you've tried setting an alarm and describing your feelings when the alarm sounded, now also rate their intensity. Doing this regularly will make you more aware of the typical intensity of your feelings. It will also help you gain insight into times and situations that produce strong feelings in you, both pleasant and unpleasant, as well as times and situations where you feel empty or blah.

At first, labeling and rating your feelings may feel unnatural and forced. That's normal. As you practice more, it'll feel more natural, and you'll begin to notice that you're more aware of your feelings even when you aren't trying to monitor them. As you become more aware of how you typically feel and the situations that trigger your feelings, you'll be one step closer to managing your feelings! This awareness will position you to respond rather than react to feelings, as we'll explain in the following section.

RESPONDING TO YOUR SIGNS

You have seen that feelings are signs telling you where you're at and what's coming ahead. You also have learned strategies to identify, label, and rate your feelings; this positions you to *respond* rather than *react* to feelings. What's the difference between responding and reacting? Reactions are quick, impulsive actions that you take without thinking. Reactions are driven by feelings. For example, when a sharp needle pricks your arm, you feel pain and immediately *react* to the pain by pulling your arm away. Responses are thoughtful, intentional actions that align with your goals, values, and desired outcomes. Responses are driven by thoughts. To continue the example, when you get an injection for administering a vaccine or taking a blood sample, a sharp needle pricks your arm, but you *respond* to the pain by keeping still, even though it hurts, because the needle is intended to help keep you safe and healthy in the long term. See the difference?

In this section, we'll focus on how you react and respond to your feelings. Before looking closely at what you typically do, let's look at how some other teens reacted and responded in situations.

Jordan likes playing video games online with his friends. He's good at it, better than most of his friends, and he reminds them how good he is when they're playing. Yesterday he was in the middle of a game with three of his friends. Just as the game was getting interesting, Jordan lost. His friends quickly piled on and teased him for losing, making him look silly in front of everyone who was part of the game. Jordan felt embarrassed and ashamed about losing, and also angry that his friends seemed to enjoy rubbing it in his face. His feelings thermometer was at a 5—intense! He told them the game was stupid and he didn't want to play it anymore, then quickly logged off. His friends texted him and asked him to come back, but he ignored them. When he didn't respond, they texted again and called him a sore loser. Jordan thought if they teased him like that they weren't really his friends, and he was better off not having "fake friends." His feelings shifted from angry and embarrassed to sad and alone.

Riley was hanging out with her friends on a Saturday night. There was a party happening at the house of someone they knew from school, and they decided to go check it out. When they got to the house and walked in, Riley saw her boyfriend on a couch talking and flirting with someone else. How could he do that to her? Riley felt betrayed, furious, and heartbroken all at the same time. Her feelings thermometer jumped from 2 to 5 in an instant! Riley began yelling at her boyfriend and hitting him in front of everyone. It took three people to pull her off of him. Then Riley ran outside crying and demanded to go home. Her friends tried to console her, but when Riley got home she immediately went to her room and slammed the door behind her. Hurt and crying, she began scratching her wrists until they bled.

As he came home from school and made his way to the fridge to grab a snack, Darian threw his hoodie over a chair. His mom muttered something about his "never putting things in their place" and picked up his hoodie to hang it in the closet. As she grabbed the hoodie, one of the sleeves got caught on the chair, and a small bag of marijuana fell out of the pocket and onto the floor. Darian froze like a statue while his mom yelled at him and said he was no good and would never amount to anything. He could hear what she was saying, but it didn't feel real to him. It was like he was in a dream. When he snapped back to reality, his mom was yelling at him to answer her, but he didn't know what to say. She snatched his phone off the counter and said he was grounded for a month. Darian felt rejected and unloved, between 4 and 5 on the feelings thermometer. He thought his mom didn't understand what he was going through and probably wished he had never been born. Darian just wanted to escape life. When he got to his room, he took three prescription pain pills he had hidden in his drawer. He wanted to numb his emotional pain and fall asleep, and he hoped he wouldn't ever wake up.

Jessica was in her room listening to music when she decided to look at recent pictures on her phone. As she looked at herself in the pictures, she felt growing discomfort about her appearance. She especially hated how big her thighs looked! Why did all her weight go directly to her thighs? What began as discomfort grew into a feeling of disgust at herself. She remembered her dad commenting that she had put on weight, and that made her feel even worse. Jessica closed the pictures but couldn't stop thinking about how bad she looked and how disgusted she felt. No matter how hard she tried to not think about it, the pictures and upset feelings wouldn't go away. She began crying in her bed and eventually fell asleep.

Jordan, Riley, Darian, and Jessica all experienced difficult situations. Those situations resulted in painful and intense negative feelings. What they felt was normal and predictable—most people would feel the way they did! Trying to change the way they felt, their immediate emotions in the moment, would be almost impossible. Remember that feelings, or emotions, are automatic and happen without our choosing to experience them. But even though in-the-moment emotions are automatic, there are things you can do to respond to your emotions that will help you manage how you feel and think over longer periods—in other words, your lasting moods. Emotions, as we have seen, are automatic feelings related to something specific that happens to you or in your environment. They usually last for only seconds or minutes. Moods are longer periods of feelings that can last hours or days. Moods are less connected to something specific that happens, like an argument.

None of the reactions of Jordan, Riley, Darian, or Jessica addressed the problems they were facing. Instead, their immediate and ineffective reactions prolonged the existing problems and in some cases made matters worse by creating new, additional problems, leading to longer periods of negative moods. That's what typically happens when we react—old problems continue and new problems arise.

Now consider the alternative: responding. Remember that responses are thoughtful, intentional actions that align with your values, goals, and desired outcomes. (Sneak preview: chapter 7 includes activities to help you identify and develop your values and goals in life—consider checking out that chapter sooner than later!)

Now let's look at several helpful strategies for making the move from reacting to responding.

Strategy #1: Buy Time

Before reacting quickly, hit the pause button and slow things down. Buying time before engaging is helpful because it allows the intensity of your in-the-moment emotions to decrease. Remember, you can't control your immediate emotional reactions to a situation, but emotional reactions typically last for only a few seconds to a few minutes. By hitting the pause button before engaging, the emotional intensity decreases (your feeling thermometer level drops), you can identify what you're feeling, and you can think more clearly about your values, goals, and desired outcomes in the situation. That allows you to be thoughtful in choosing a response. The more you practice responding, the more natural and automatic it becomes. That means you won't need to pause or take breaks as much before responding, although it's still a good idea to step back from situations before engaging if your feelings thermometer tends to shoot to 4 or 5.

Strategy #2: Breathe

While you're buying time, breathe! Sounds simple, right? You've been doing it since you were born. So how can breathing help you move from reacting to responding? Think about what happens to your breathing when you experience negative feelings at 5 on the feelings thermometer. When you're at 5, your body goes into fight-or-flight mode because it thinks you're in danger. Your body prepares to take action to defend yourself or escape. When you're in fight-or-flight mode, your heart beats rapidly, your muscles tense, and your breathing becomes shallow and rapid, sending blood and oxygen to your muscles quickly so you can fight or run away. Your body directs all its resources to taking action instead of to the parts of your brain needed for careful thought. This is super helpful if a bear is chasing you, but if you're sitting in your classroom or hanging out with friends, it's really not.

What you need to do in those situations is calm your body down so it redirects resources to the parts of your brain that allow you to think carefully and make good decisions. That's where breathing comes in! By slowing down your breathing, you can make your body shift out of fight-or-flight mode and get into a headspace that will allow you to respond thoughtfully.

There are many different breathing techniques. We like to start with a technique called *belly breathing*. To belly breathe, place one hand on your belly and the other hand on your chest. Close your mouth and slowly breathe in through your nose, silently counting to four as you breathe in. As you breathe in, keep your chest still and let your belly push your hand out. Then slowly breathe out through your mouth, again silently counting to four. Feel your hand and belly move in as you breathe out, again keeping your chest still. Belly breathing works best if you sit or lie down, but you can also do it standing if you need to. Some people find it more relaxing to close their eyes when belly breathing, but that's up to you, too.

Repeat belly breathing five to ten times. Feel your hand and belly move out each time you slowly inhale through your nose and move in each time you slowly exhale through your mouth. Pay attention to how you feel as you're breathing.

How do you feel now? If more relaxed and calm, that's great—you're on your way to managing your feelings! If you don't feel more relaxed yet, that's okay. For most people, it takes several tries before they notice the benefits of belly breathing. If you don't feel more relaxed yet, keep practicing it a couple of times a day for the next week. Belly breathing may be most helpful when you're feeling tense or upset, but we recommend you practice it a couple of times a day regardless of how you're feeling, at least until you've reached a point where it helps you relax quickly. A great thing about belly breathing is you can practice it discreetly almost anywhere, including at home, in class, sitting in traffic, and so on.

As you practice, make a note of where you're at on the feelings thermometer before you start and when you finish. This will help you identify how helpful belly breathing is for you. If belly breathing doesn't seem to help you relax, try a different breathing technique, like square breathing. In square breathing, you breathe deeply while counting to four, pause your breath until the count of four, breathe out while counting to four, and then pause again until the count of four. There's nothing magical about the number four—three, five, or another number might work better for you. Give it a try and find what helps you relax most! Search the internet for other breathing techniques, try them out, and find the one that works best for you.

Strategy #3: Accept Your Feelings

Wait, what? Accept your feelings? Maybe you're thinking you don't want to accept your feelings because some of them are really painful, scary, or upsetting. That's a common reaction when people are introduced to the idea of acceptance. But accepting your feelings probably isn't what you first think it is. Accepting your feelings doesn't mean approving of them, allowing them to control you, or giving up on feeling better. It also doesn't mean accepting bad situations that you can change, like if someone is mistreating you. You definitely shouldn't accept being mistreated! Accepting in this context means being aware that you're experiencing a feeling but not judging the feeling as good or bad, and not trying to change the feeling in the moment. It means observing the feeling and allowing it to be, just as it is.

Why would that be helpful? If you don't like negative feelings (and who does?), what's the point of accepting them?

To start answering that question, reflect on what you typically do when you experience negative feelings. If you're like most people, you probably try to get rid of the bad feeling, push it away, or deny it's even there. You resist and reject the bad feeling. It's a normal reaction to avoid bad feelings at all costs.

Does it work? Nope. The more you try to push a feeling away or suppress it, the stickier it becomes. When that happens, sometimes people push even harder to get rid of the feeling by doing things like abusing substances to dampen the feeling or cutting themselves to produce different feelings. That's what Darian and Riley did. But none of those actions make bad feelings go away for long. They just come back.

To illustrate this point, try a silly experiment. Set a timer for one minute on your phone or watch. For that one minute, try as hard as you can to *not* think about a pink penguin.

How'd it go? Couldn't get that pink penguin out of your mind, could you? By trying hard to not think about something, you're actually putting more attention on it and making it stick in your head. That's true not only for pink penguins but also for suicidal thoughts. The same happens with feelings. If you become focused on trying to not feel something, it gets sticky, and you're going to feel it even more.

So, because trying to push bad feelings away doesn't work, try something else! When you experience a bad feeling, name it. For example, say to yourself, *Sad...I am feeling sad.* Instead of pushing sadness away, sit back and visualize sadness as a wave that flows through you, without judging it or fighting against it. Sadness comes and goes. You are not sadness; sadness is something you experience. Sadness and other feelings are normal parts of life. When you try to force negative emotions away, you'll find yourself stuck in a repeating cycle of experiencing them, trying to suppress them, but having them come right back. Then negative feelings control you. But by accepting negative feelings as a part of your human experience, you escape that cycle, and you're empowered to make a choice about how you'll respond to feelings, instead of allowing them to control you.

Returning to an earlier point: does accepting negative feelings mean you're throwing in the towel on feeling better? Not at all! Ironically, accepting negative feelings actually leads to feeling better overall. This happens in part because accepting negative feelings makes them less sticky, allowing them to go away faster. What's more, even though positive feelings are great, it's not realistic to expect to experience only positive feelings in life. Negative feelings exist for a reason—they're a natural response to bad experiences. A key to a better life is not to get rid of negative feelings, but to learn how to cope with them effectively. Practicing acceptance, along with the other strategies in this book, will allow you to do just that!

Strategy #4: Adopt a Different Perspective

The way we see things—that is, our *perspective*—greatly influences how we think and feel about them. In photography, forced perspective refers to the use of techniques to create an illusion that something is smaller or larger than it really is. You've probably seen pictures that used forced perspective, where people appear to hold the sun in the palm of their hand, rest their foot on top of a pyramid, or support the leaning Tower of Pisa with their back. Maybe you've used forced perspective yourself. Forced perspective uses your understanding of the scale and size of objects to trick your brain into thinking something in the picture is smaller or larger than it really is. It illustrates the power of perspective. Things can look very different if we change the position from which we view them!

The same principle applies to your understandings of feelings and situations. The way you feel and think about a situation can change if you look at it from a different perspective. When you're in the middle of a situation, there's a lot of information to process: what's happening in your environment, what's happening inside of you, and the back-and-forth between your environment and internal experiences. That's a lot to keep track of! What's more, the intensity of your emotional experiences can make it more difficult to process all the information and make thoughtful decisions.

When you step back from a situation and think about it as if it were happening to someone else, you can adopt a more objective perspective and see more clearly what's happening in your environment. That's why we ask friends, teachers, or counselors to help us navigate through difficult situations. They can see things more clearly and objectively because they are not in the middle of the situation.

Although talking to others is helpful and sometimes even necessary, you can experience some of the same benefits simply by adopting a different perspective. When you're experiencing strong feelings and having difficulty knowing what to do, step back for a minute and envision someone else being in your situation. For example, if you've been bullied and you're feeling hurt, resentful, and unsure what to do, imagine it was another teen in the same situation instead of you. Close your eyes, become an outside observer, and visualize another person in your situation. This allows you to detach yourself from the intensity of the situation and view it more like an outsider—to adopt a different perspective. As you do so, you'll likely find that your feelings become less intense and that you're able to think more clearly about how to respond to the situation.

Give it a try! In your journal, write down a challenging experience you're having, such as getting a bad grade, feeling lonely and disconnected from others, or arguing with your caregivers. If you can't think of any happening right now, pick an experience that happened in the last month. Now imagine it was your friend going through that experience instead of you. Close your eyes, become an outside observer, and visualize your friend in the experience. Does the emotional intensity feel as high when you're viewing someone else in the situation? What advice would you give your friend on how to respond? Write down what you would say to your friend. Now consider how you can apply that advice to your own situation.

These four strategies—buying time, breathing, accepting your feelings, and adopting a different perspective—will help you manage your feelings and prepare you to respond instead of react. In describing these strategies, we've focused mainly on managing your difficult, negative feelings. It's also important to identify when you experience positive feelings. Becoming more aware of your positive feelings will help you develop a more balanced view of your emotional experiences. It will also position you to use strategies to promote and prolong your positive experiences.

Strategy #5: Savor Positive Feelings

We've talked about how people can get stuck in negative thoughts and feelings, and we've offered some tips for getting unstuck. But what if you could get stuck in positive thoughts and feelings? Wouldn't that be great? This fifth strategy, called savoring, will help you do that.

To savor means to taste and enjoy something completely. Typically we use the word *savor* to talk about deeply enjoying food that we like (the word *savor* actually comes from a Latin word meaning "to taste"). When you're preparing to eat your favorite dessert, you may breathe in deeply to smell it, take small bites, and chew it slowly, moving it around in your mouth before swallowing to enjoy the wonderful taste. That's savoring! It prolongs and maximizes the pleasant experience of eating that dessert.

Savoring isn't limited to desserts (or other foods). You can also use it with your positive feelings. Remember that positive feelings are a part of life to be accepted, just like negative feelings. When you get stressed out and upset, your thoughts and attention get pulled to negative feelings, thoughts, and memories. This creates an imbalance, an overemphasis on negative parts of life. You can use savoring to increase your positive experiences and create more balance.

Think about a time when you were really happy or at peace. Maybe it was enjoying a beautiful scene in nature, hanging out with your closest friends, a family vacation you took, or cuddling with your pet. It doesn't matter what the event was; what matters is that you experienced it very positively and enjoyed it deeply. If you find it difficult to recall a "big" event, that's okay. Focus on a small event from the past week, like the positive feelings of a warm shower, a laugh you shared with someone, or a pretty sunset you saw.

Get in a comfortable position, close your eyes, and picture your pleasant event in your mind as vividly as possible. Try to recall as many details as possible—the sounds, the smells, the sights, and all the sensations you experienced, including what you felt inside. Stay in that moment for several minutes, being aware of and appreciating the sensations and feelings in the pleasant event.

After savoring, write down your pleasant memories in your journal so that you can come back to them later. As with any other activity, you'll get better at savoring with practice. Try savoring once a day for the next week and see if you feel more positive and relaxed after doing it. Some people find it helpful to savor positive memories right before going to bed, as it helps them relax and end the day on a positive note.

In addition to savoring pleasant memories from the past, you can also use savoring to maximize pleasant experiences in the present and future. To apply savoring to the present, when you're having a pleasant experience, focus on being present and aware of all the sensations—sights, sounds, smells, and feelings. This will deepen your enjoyment of the moment and build a stronger memory for this pleasant experience. To apply savoring to the future, focus on an upcoming pleasant event and visualize it as you would a pleasant memory. For example, if you're planning to go to the movies with a friend on Friday night, visualize the experience: the smell of popcorn, the sounds of the movie, the feeling of the dark, cool theater, and so on. Enjoy the positive sensations even before the event happens!

A final way to use savoring is to shift away from sticky negative feelings. This can be a little harder and takes more practice. When you're feeling down, stressed, or upset, go back to your journal and find a pleasant memory you've written down. Visualize and savor the pleasant event, using it as a way to transition from negative to positive feelings.

APPLICATION

Now that you have learned some strategies that are helpful in moving from reacting to responding, let's return to Jordan, Riley, Darian, and Jessica. Think about some ways they might have used these strategies to respond to the difficult situations they encountered. Here are some possible responses and their results, based on each teen's values and desired outcomes.

Jordan valued his friendships. What he wanted in the situation was to have fun playing games with friends and for them to stop teasing him. How could he have responded? He recognized that he felt embarrassed and ashamed about losing, and angry about being teased. If his feelings were too intense to respond thoughtfully in the moment, he could have bought himself time by telling his friends he was taking a break from the game and would be back. During his break, he could go to a quiet place in his house and use belly breathing to relax and cool his emotions. He could remind himself that he brags about winning and sometimes teases his friends, too. He doesn't mean to hurt their feelings when he does that, so they probably didn't mean to hurt his feelings when they did it to him. After a few minutes, his feelings thermometer drops from 5 to 3. Feeling less upset, he could return to the game and find that he's soon having fun again. This way he maintains his friendships and returns to having fun playing games with them—a much better outcome than when he reacted by calling the game stupid and isolating himself from his friends.

Riley valued her dignity, social reputation, and relationships with others. What she wanted in the situation was to make her boyfriend understand how much his action hurt her, maintain her dignity in front of peers from school, and receive support from her friends. She felt betrayed, furious, and heartbroken. If she was too upset to respond thoughtfully in the moment, she could defuse the situation by asking her friends to go outside with her away from the crowd of people (that is, buy some time). Once outside, she could talk to her friends about how upset she is, which would bring about support from her friends. She also could ask her friends to help her decide how to respond. Asking friends is a variation on adopting a different perspective—instead of envisioning how someone else could respond to this situation, Riley was able to directly ask her friends for advice on how to respond. Problem solving with friends would allow her to identify exactly what she wanted to say to her boyfriend, as well as how and when she wanted to say it. For example, maybe confronting him privately instead of in front of a large group of people at the party would be more consistent with her desired outcome. Although she's still hurt and upset, after she goes outside and problem solves with her friends, her feelings thermometer drops from 5 to 3 or 4. Riley is calmer and now has a plan for handling this difficult situation, one that maintains her relationships with her friends, her dignity, and her social reputation.

Darian valued his relationship with his mother, even though they didn't always get along. He didn't want to disappoint her or make her life harder. What he wanted was to feel understood, supported, and loved by her. If he felt panicked and frozen in the moment, he obviously wasn't ready to engage in a difficult conversation. His mom's upset feelings and intensity were a sign that she wasn't in a good place to engage in a productive conversation either. Instead of shutting down and turning to substances to escape the pain, Darian could have asked for time by saying something like, "I know you're upset, Mom. I'm upset, too, and I just can't think clearly right now. I need to collect myself so we can talk about this later tonight."

Then he could use a strategy that helps him soothe and think more clearly: going for a run in his neighborhood. While running, Darian practices accepting his upset feelings. He pictures his upset feelings as a wave that flows through him, without judging them or fighting against them. This allows him to remember that upset feelings are a normal part of life and that he is still in control of his actions even when he experiences them. This doesn't make the upset feelings disappear, but they become less intense. After running and showering, Darian still feels nervous about talking to his mom, but his feeling thermometer is at 3 instead of 5. He's now in a better place to hear what his mom says, tell her about the difficult thoughts and feelings he has been experiencing, and ask her for help. She, too, is in a calmer, better place to express her thoughts and listen to Darian. His response leads to an important, although difficult, conversation with his mom, which leaves him feeling more understood, supported, and loved by her, and also understanding better why his mom was upset about his marijuana use.

Jessica's challenging situation differed from the others because it didn't involve conflict with other people. Instead, her situation arose from internal experiences: the thoughts and feelings she experienced when looking at pictures of herself. Jessica *wanted* to value herself, but she struggled to accept her body. Instead of trying to suppress her thoughts and feelings of disgust and sadness, she could have adopted another perspective, by envisioning her friend in the same situation. She would tell her friend that her value as a person is unrelated to her body and she is loved and accepted for who she is. She also would remind her friend of all her positive qualities. Then Jessica could pivot to another strategy: savoring positive memories. She found a picture taken when celebrating her birthday with her closest friends—a very positive event! She closed her eyes and pictured her birthday in her mind, focusing on her friends singing to her, the sound and feeling of her laughing as they sang off-key, and how happy and at peace she felt talking with them far into the night. Jessica drifted off to sleep with these positive memories on her mind, feeling calmer and less upset.

The experiences of Jordan, Riley, Darian, and Jessica are common for teens. Maybe you've had similar experiences yourself. Think about how you typically react to difficult situations where your feelings thermometer reaches 5 for negative feelings like sadness, anger, and fear. In what ways do you react similarly to Jordan, Riley, Darian, or Jessica? We each have our own way of reacting, but some common reactions are verbally lashing out at others, breaking or throwing things, eating too much to distract from painful feelings, using substances to numb the pain, and shutting down and isolating from others.

Responding requires that you identify what you're feeling, resist the urge to immediately react to the feeling, and come up with a thoughtful plan that aligns with your values. If you're thinking that responding sounds hard, you're right! It's hard because it requires you to override your immediate impulses and change something you've been doing for a long time. And the main reason you have been doing it is that it feels right in the moment. Lashing out in anger, using substances, or cutting or hurting yourself might momentarily dampen your pain, but as you saw in the examples, the temporary relief almost always leads to continued and bigger problems in the long run. In contrast, thoughtful responding addresses the pain you're feeling in the moment and results in better outcomes in the future.

Even though responding is hard, you can do it! Like any other challenge, it requires being intentional. The more you practice it, the more natural it will become.

MOVING FORWARD

In this chapter, you've learned strategies for reading and responding to your emotions. You've learned tips to identify, label, and rate your feelings. Once you've developed awareness of what you're feeling, you're ready to take steps to manage your feelings. You've also learned the important distinction between reacting and responding, as well as the short- and long-term benefits of thoughtfully responding to feelings. You've picked up some useful strategies to promote thoughtful responding, including buying time, breathing exercises, accepting your feelings, and adopting a different perspective. You've also learned a new strategy to promote and prolong pleasant feelings: savoring.

As you move on from this chapter, practice these strategies for managing your feelings regularly. With regular practice, they'll begin to feel automatic and will become your default way of managing feelings.

In the next chapter, you'll work on challenging your negative thoughts and learn some skills for managing them and turning them in a more positive direction.

CHAPTER 4

Identifying and Managing Negative Thoughts

Your thoughts are like a navigation system as you journey through life. But which thoughts should you listen to? To get where you want to go in life, you need accurate and healthy ways of thinking. That's the focus of this chapter. You'll learn to identify common thinking patterns that contribute to thoughts of suicide, called *thinking traps*. Then you'll learn strategies to sidestep those traps, talk back to hurtful thoughts, and develop more healthy ways of thinking. The strategies don't include "Just think happy thoughts" or "Pretend everything's fine when it's really not." That's not helpful or realistic. Instead, the strategies will allow you to think flexibly and turn down the volume when the negative voice gets loud.

THINKING STYLES

The way you typically think about things—positively or negatively—can become a habit or a style. You probably have a thinking style, even if you don't realize it. Your thinking style becomes a problem if it's inflexible, meaning you view things the same way regardless of the circumstances. There are always multiple ways to think about situations, yourself, or your future. If the way you've been thinking isn't going so well—maybe you're feeling upset much of the time and thinking about giving up on life—some changes can open the door to feeling better.

How you think about things is important because it directly influences how you feel (and vice versa). To flesh out this point, grab your journal and try this exercise (Curry et al., 2005). The table shown here lists some example situations and two very different ways of thinking about them. In your journal, write down a feeling that matches each way of thinking. Imagine yourself in the situation and having the different thoughts: How might you feel? To get you started, we've completed the first one.

What happened	What I thought	How I feel
You get a C on a test.	A. I'll never get into college.	Worried
	B. Phew—I thought for sure I failed that test!	Relieved
A friend passes in the hall and doesn't look at or speak to you.	A. They're avoiding me because they don't like me.	
	B. They're preoccupied about something.	
Your best friend asks someone else to hang out.	A. They're don't want to be my friend anymore.	
	B. They're so friendly with everyone.	
Your teacher wants to speak with you after class.	A. I must be in trouble.	
	B. They really liked my work.	
Your parent is late to pick you up.	A. They must have had a car accident.	
	B. Traffic must be bad today.	

What happened	What I thought	How I feel
You get second place in the science fair.	A. The judges don't think my project is good enough.	
	B. The judges are impressed by my project!	
The cafeteria is out of brownies by the time you go through the line.	A. I never get good things.	
	B. I was too late to get a brownie today, but I'll try again tomorrow.	

What did you learn from this exercise? Different ways of thinking about situations, yourself, and your future produce different feelings! We intentionally provided extremely different thoughts for each situation to emphasize this point, but even small differences in how you think can influence your feelings.

We didn't ask you to think about what you would *do* in these situations (your actions), but how different thoughts might make you *feel*. Different thoughts and feelings can lead to different actions. For example, in the situation *The cafeteria is out of brownies by the time you go through the line,* the thought *I never get good things* leads to passive acceptance of not getting what you want. By contrast, the thought *I was too late to get a brownie today, but I'll try again tomorrow* could lead you to taking helpful action: *I'll go earlier tomorrow to make sure I get one.* Even though that's a simple example that doesn't involve complicated relationships or strong emotions, it illustrates how your thoughts, feelings, and actions are connected. Because they're connected, changing the way you think can change how you feel and act. Let's see how you usually think and if there are some areas you would like to change.

Look back at the exercise you just completed. Each situation provided two thoughts—option A and option B. Does one of the two options sound more like the voice in your head? If it's option A, your thinking style tends toward the negative. Negative thinking styles are glass-half-empty; they gravitate toward expecting the worst in situations, being self-critical, and being pessimistic about the future. If it's option B, your thinking style leans positive. Positive thinking styles are glass-half-full; they gravitate toward expecting the best in situations, thinking favorably about yourself, and being optimistic about the future. If the voice in your head was more like option A for some examples and option B for others, then your thinking style is probably characterized by a mix of positive and negative thoughts.

Flexibility is valuable when it comes to how you think about things. That's because your thinking needs to be grounded and informed by relevant details in situations and circumstances. It's not healthy to think the same way in every situation. If you always think negatively, you'll have an unrealistically sour view of life and miss out on good things! You'll also feel pretty miserable. If you always think positively, you'll also be unrealistic and inaccurate—missing out on relevant cues alerting you to problems and guiding you to change your actions. When your thinking is always negative or always positive, your feelings and actions will often be inappropriate for the situation. Instead, you need a balanced, flexible thinking style informed by relevant situational details, including the good and the bad.

Imagine that you and your friends text each other and decide to go see a movie. You're going to walk to meet them at the theater. As you open the front door and step outside, you see dark clouds in the sky. There are three possible scenarios:

- **Scenario 1:** The voice in your head says, *Those clouds look bad. It's going to storm. I'll get soaked if I walk to the theater.* You decide to stay home. You feel bored and bummed out.

- **Scenario 2:** The voice in your head says, *No big deal. I can't wait to see the movie!* You rush out the door. Before you reach the end of the block, it begins to pour. You arrive at the theater drenched and freezing. You try to enjoy the movie, but you feel miserable because you can't stop shivering.

- **Scenario 3:** The voice in your head says, *It's probably going to rain, but I really want to see this movie with my friends. I'd better grab my raincoat and umbrella just in case.* It begins to pour before you reach the end of the block, but you arrive at the theater dry because you're wearing your coat and carrying an umbrella. You enjoy watching the movie with your friends.

Do you see how different ways of thinking resulted in different actions and feelings? In scenario 1, your overly negative focus on something bad happening prevented you from focusing on the positive of watching the movie with your friends. You stayed dry, but you missed out on a good time! In scenario 2, your overly positive focus on having a good time prevented you from recognizing the looming threat of rain and taking appropriate actions to stay dry. You made it to the movie, but you didn't enjoy it because you were cold and wet! In scenario 3, you focused on both the looming threat and the good time. That balanced view of negative and positive allowed you to take appropriate actions to stay dry and go to the movie. Balanced and flexible thinking that recognizes all aspects of a situation—positive and negative—produces better outcomes.

Identifying Your Thinking Style

Now let's focus on your thoughts. This exercise is about gathering evidence of your thinking style by identifying the thoughts you have. To start, write down in your journal one stressful event or challenging situation that happened last week. Try to recall what you thought when the event happened. Write down what you remember about your thoughts at the time. If you remember multiple stressful events in the last week, try to recall and write down what you were thinking for as many events as possible.

If you can't remember any stressful events from last week, that's okay, because you're going to keep a log of stressful events in the coming week. Keeping track of how you think in stressful situations will help you develop a better understanding of your thinking style. Pay attention to when your feelings change suddenly, and ask yourself what goes through your mind in those moments. When your feelings change suddenly, that's an ideal time to grab your journal and identify and evaluate your thoughts. There's almost always a thought connected to your change in feelings.

Another revealing time to identify the voice in your head is when you experience thoughts of suicide. Your negative voice often gets loud right before you have thoughts of suicide. Pay close attention to the voice in your head just before the thoughts of suicide started, and write down what it was saying in your journal. Identifying what you're thinking when you experience sudden emotional shifts and suicidal thoughts can provide valuable insight into your thinking style. More important, it can point toward what you can change to manage your feelings and turn down the volume on the negative voice that triggers suicidal thoughts.

As you collect your thoughts in your journal over the next week, see if you can identify recurring themes or patterns. Do you tend to view situations as mostly negative? Can you tell what thinking style you might use most often? In your journal, write about what you notice.

Common Thinking Traps

There are ways of thinking that commonly trigger thoughts of suicide. We call these thinking traps because it's easy to get caught in them and hard to get out. Let's look at some of these common thinking traps and how you can side-step them.

Consider what happens when some creature gets caught in a physical trap. It realizes it's in a bad situation and may think there's no way out. Maybe it views the pain of the trap as unbearable and gives up hope of ever getting out. The same thing can happen to us when we get caught in thinking traps. We can come to believe we're stuck a terrible situation, the emotional pain is unbearable, there's no hope of its ever getting better, and the only escape is suicide.

The following are common thinking traps that can snare you and trigger thoughts of suicide.

- *Thinking something is much worse than it actually is.* This is called *catastrophizing* because it blows things so out of proportion that they seem like catastrophes. You can catastrophize about a situation you're in, something that happened in the past, or something that might happen in the future. Catastrophizing brings about strong negative feelings and pushes you toward hopelessness that can trigger suicidal thoughts. For example:

  - Because the person I asked out turned me down, I can't ever show my face at school again.

  - My mom yelled at me this morning, so now the whole day will be ruined.

  - Not being selected for the band is so awful I should kill myself.

  - I got a bad grade on my homework, so I'll never be successful.

- *Thinking in extremes.* This is called *all-or-nothing thinking* because it doesn't recognize middle ground or in-between points. When you engage in all-or-nothing thinking, situations are either all good or all bad, all right or all wrong, wonderful or terrible. This extreme thinking puts you on an emotional roller coaster that leads you to act in ways that don't match the reality of situations. It also can lead you to believe that emotional pain is unbearable and suicide is the only solution. All-or-nothing thinking sounds like the following:

- If I don't get first place, I'm a complete failure.

- If I can't feel happy all the time, I'd rather be dead.

- Because my friend said something that hurt my feelings, he's a bad person.

- Because my boyfriend and I had an argument, our relationship is awful.

- *Jumping to conclusions.* Jumping to conclusions is assuming things will go bad when there's no evidence to support this. One type of jumping to conclusions is *mind reading.* Mind reading is assuming you know what other people are thinking. Jumping to conclusions and mind reading can lead you to feel and act in ways that aren't appropriate to the situation. If you believe in advance that a situation will go badly, then you may avoid the situation or not put forth an effort. That makes it more likely that the situation actually will go badly. If you assume someone doesn't like you, you may experience negative feelings and change the way you act around them. That makes it more likely that they may really start to dislike you. Jumping to conclusions sounds like this:

- If other teens see me sitting alone, they'll think I'm a loser.

- There's no point in talking to them, because I already know what they'll say.

- If my romantic partner doesn't reply to my text immediately, they must not like me, and our relationship will fail.

- My teacher gave me a bad grade—they hate me.

- *Denying positive experiences.* This is called *discounting the positive.* This isn't only overlooking and ignoring good things, but taking it a step further and coming up with ways to explain away good things as not true or important. You can deny positive things that happen in life and positive things about yourself. Discounting the positive sucks the joy out of life and feeds into hopelessness because it makes life seem bleak. Also, if you find yourself saying, "Yes, but…" after something good happens, you're probably discounting the positive! Discounting the positive sounds like this:

  - I got an A on a test. It doesn't mean I'm smart; I got lucky.

  - Even though I feel better lately, my suicidal thoughts are going to come back.

  - Janie complimented my hair. She's such a liar.

  - Danny invited me to a party. He doesn't like me; he just feels sorry for me.

- *Demanding perfection.* Perfectionism is a surefire way to be unhappy. When you set impossible standards for yourself, you'll never be able to meet them, so you'll never be good enough. Perfectionism doesn't allow you to enjoy life because it keeps you focused on what you don't have (the perfect) instead of the good things you do have. It can leave you feeling trapped and unable to make your life better. Perfectionism sounds like this:

  - I'm a failure because I missed three questions on a hundred-question test.

  - I want to die because my social media post didn't get as many "likes" as someone else's.

  - I quit dance because if I can't do it perfectly, I won't do it at all.

  - If my clothes don't look just right, people will think I'm a total loser.

- *Playing the blame game.* This thinking trap involves unfairly blaming yourself for things that are outside of your control. Of course, sometimes things *are* your fault. But situations usually involve many factors, only some of which are under your control. Playing the blame game results in your feeling guilty and inadequate much of the time. A variation of the blame game is *personalization:* believing that what others say or do is directly connected to you when it really isn't. Then you feel offended, neglected, or upset for no reason.

  - My family is always upset because of me. They'd be better off if I were dead.

  - My girlfriend's entree was undercooked. It's my fault because I picked the restaurant.

  - Two guys in class are snickering. They must be making fun of me.

  - My dad plays the radio too loud when he drops me off at school. He does it on purpose to embarrass me.

In your journal, write down each of the thinking traps just described:

- Catastrophizing

- All-or-nothing thinking

- Jumping to conclusions

- Discounting the positive

- Demanding perfection

- Playing the blame game

Then circle the ones you've gotten caught in. If you can recall specific examples of when you've been caught in a thinking trap, write them down in your journal, too. Some people find writing down their negative thoughts seems to neutralize them or remove the sting. Sometimes thoughts don't seem as bad or upsetting once we put them in writing. However, focusing on negative thoughts can be painful and feel overwhelming at times. If you feel upset as you reflect on thinking traps, take a break and use the strategies for managing your feelings that you learned in chapter 3.

Keep in mind what you learned in chapter 1: thoughts change! Just because you've gotten caught in thinking traps in the past doesn't mean you'll always get caught in them. And if you do get caught again, it doesn't mean you're a failure. Learn from the experience so you'll be less likely to get caught again! You can use the tips in the rest of this chapter to identify and sidestep thinking traps. By doing so, you'll develop more flexible and accurate ways of thinking about yourself, the world, and your future, which will put you on the path to a more positive and hope-filled life.

SIDESTEP THINKING TRAPS

In this section, we'll present tips for sidestepping common thinking traps. Some traps may be more relevant to you than others, so focus intently on the tips for sidestepping the traps that you fall into regularly. But even if you don't fall into a particular thinking trap often, you can still benefit from using all these tips, because they'll help keep your thoughts sharp, accurate, and trap-free!

Decatastrophize

As you've read, catastrophizing means blowing things out of proportion in a negative way. Catastrophizing is one of the most common thinking traps. It induces a sense of despair—a belief that life is terrible! Catastrophizing can feel like a runaway train, gaining momentum as the negative voice barrels through your head. If you believe things are terrible, you'll feel upset and possibly hopeless, and maybe think the only option is to end your life.

Bad things happen. Sometimes even terrible things happen. But most experiences aren't nearly as bad as catastrophizing would have you believe. So how can you stop the runaway catastrophizing train before it leaves the station? Start by writing down the negative thought. Reflect on the thought for a moment and then ask yourself *What evidence supports this thought, and what evidence contradicts it?* Write down evidence for and against your thought.

Next, ask yourself *How probable is it that this negative thought is true?* and write down a number from 0 (not true at all) to 100 (absolutely true) beside the thought. Keep in mind the distinction between probable and possible. Many things are possible, meaning there's a chance they could be true. But just because something is possible doesn't mean it's true or that it's definitely going to happen. It's *possible* you'll get struck by lightning or win the lottery, but it's very, very unlikely. Probable means it's likely true or the chances are high that it'll happen. It's easy to spend a lot of time and energy on negative thoughts with a tiny probability of being true or happening. By stopping yourself and differentiating what's probable from what's possible, you'll get a better handle on how realistic your negative thoughts are. And if they aren't probable, you can come up with alternative thoughts that are more probable.

Finally, ask yourself, *If this thought is, in fact, true, what's the worst that could happen? And if the worst did happen, what could I do to cope?* Many people find that after writing down the worst-case scenario, it's not as bad as they originally expected. The worst-case scenario may be unpleasant, unsatisfying, embarrassing, painful, and so on. But it's rarely as catastrophic as the negative voice makes it seem. Further, generating a list of ways you could cope with the worst-case scenario produces a sense of calm confidence that you can handle whatever comes your way.

Let's see how decatastrophizing could be applied to Tina, a teen who received a notification that her SAT scores had been posted. She felt a lump in her throat and butterflies in her stomach as she logged in to see her scores. Her math score was 100 points lower than on the most recent practice test she'd taken. Tina was devastated. As tears filled her eyes, she knew her dream of becoming a doctor was over. If she couldn't become a doctor, there was no reason to go on living.

Tina experienced a very real, disappointing setback and then catastrophized to the point that she wanted to stop living. How could Tina decatastrophize and turn things around?

1. Identify and write down my thought: *My dream of becoming a doctor is over because I scored lower than I wanted on the math section of the SAT.*

2. Evidence for my thought: *Math SAT scores are considered in admission decisions at the university I want to attend.*

3. Evidence against my thought: *Math SAT scores are only one part of university admissions decisions. I can take the SAT again and try to improve my score. Other people have scored lower on the SAT and been admitted to universities. Some universities don't even require the SAT for admission.*

4. How probable is it that this thought is true? *Ten out of a hundred. It's possible this SAT score could hurt my chances of getting into universities and eventually becoming a doctor, but there are a lot of other factors involved in becoming a doctor.*

5. What's the worst that could happen? *I don't get into my top choice university.*

6. If that happens, what could I do to cope? *I could apply to other universities and maybe attend community college for two years before transferring to the university I want to attend.*

After writing down her thought and decatastrophizing, Tina realized the situation wasn't as extreme as she had first believed. She was still disappointed in her score, but she now saw a viable path to attending a university and pursuing her dream of becoming a doctor. Tina's hopelessness turned into resolve and determination.

Be a Reporter, Not a Forecaster

Another thinking trap is jumping to conclusions. When you jump to conclusions, you assume you know how a situation will turn out in the absence of supporting evidence. The same happens with mind reading—you assume you know what other people are thinking, without any special insight into their thought processes. Often we assume situations will turn out badly before they've even happened or that other people will think bad thoughts about us. So we feel upset about things that probably won't ever happen!

When you jump to conclusions or mind read, you act like a weather forecaster, trying to predict something that may or may not happen. But unlike weather forecasters, you aren't a trained meteorologist with tons of data and mathematical models on which to base predictions (and meteorologists still get the weather wrong sometimes, despite all their data).

We all act like forecasters sometimes, even though we know it's logically impossible. As an example of how illogical it is, try the following:

• Predict the winning lottery numbers.

• Forecast the weather two weeks from today.

• Look at someone across the room and know what they're thinking at that moment.

- Pick out a face in a crowd and know their favorite ice cream flavor.

Obviously, you can't do these things. Nobody can! In the same way, you can't know for sure how future situations will turn out. You have to wait to see what happens. You can't read other people's minds. You have to wait for them to tell you what they're thinking. If you catch yourself jumping to conclusions, remind yourself to wait for the results.

Reporters tell us what's happening or has happened without trying to predict the future. They focus on facts, not possibilities. Act like a reporter, not a forecaster!

When you catch yourself getting upset about a bad outcome that hasn't happened yet or getting stressed out by what someone might be thinking, remind yourself to be a reporter. Focus on what actually happens and what you can know with certainty, and leave the fortune-telling to someone else!

Embrace the Positives

You probably know someone who sees only the negative. If you say, "It's a beautiful day" they respond, "It'll probably rain tomorrow." Maybe sometimes *you* are the person who always sees the bad side. It's a skewed and inaccurate way of thinking. Good things happen; so do bad things. To function well and feel well, you need to recognize both good and bad. You need balanced thinking.

If the voice in your head seems to point out only the negative, work toward recognizing the positives—and embracing them. You can start by keeping a log of your positive qualities and positive things that happen in your life.

What are your positive qualities? Are you organized, creative, kind? Are you a good listener, an encourager, an athlete? Are you smart, funny, generous? Are you a foodie, a gamer, a history buff? You possess all kinds of positive qualities! Write down five of your positive qualities in your journal.

Sometimes people find it difficult to identify their positive qualities. They may focus on the negatives or think it's egotistical to think of themselves in positive terms. It's not! Remember, a *balanced* way of thinking is a healthy way of thinking. This means recognizing the good and the bad. If you're having trouble coming up with five positive qualities, think about what your friends or family would list as your positive characteristics, talents, achievements, and so on. If you're still having trouble, go ahead and ask a trusted friend or adult what positive qualities they see in you—and then write them in your journal!

Now that you have a list of some of your positive qualities, keep a log of when you display those qualities. For example, if "good listener" is on your list, write down in your journal when you show that you're a good listener (for example, "I listened to my friend Gabby when she needed to vent about problems with her parents"). Make it a priority to write down at least one example of how you show your positive qualities every day. As you do so, you'll become more in touch with all the good things about you!

In addition, keep a log of positive *experiences* that happen each day. Lots of good things that happen every day go unnoticed: a smile from someone in the hallway, the smell of fresh-baked bread, the warm cozy feeling as you fall asleep, a good grade on homework, a refreshing breeze on a hot day, hot cocoa on a cold night, an engaging conversation. When you overlook these good everyday experiences, you miss out on the joy and comfort they can bring to your life. Don't miss out! Start keeping a log of positive experiences by writing down three good things that happen every day. They don't need to be huge events like winning first place in a competition or going on a date with someone you've had a crush on for years. In fact, it's better to write down experiences that seem minor, because those are the types of experiences you often overlook. By writing down these experiences daily, you'll become more aware of the enjoyable parts of life. This, in turn, will result in a more positive outlook on life. Some people find it particularly helpful to record three positive experiences right before they go to bed. This puts them in a calm, happy place as they fall asleep.

Recognizing the positives is a great way to improve your outlook and enjoy life more. Sometimes you'll also need to push back on the negative voice in your head. Do you find it hard to accept praise? Do you explain away or minimize compliments? When someone says something positive, do you find yourself thinking or saying, "Yes, but..."? If so, the negative voice in your head is trying to discount the positives. You need to push back!

First, stop explaining away compliments. Most people, most of the time, are sincere when they say something nice about you. Respond with "Thank you" and skip discounting statements like "I was lucky" or "I normally mess things up." Allow people the satisfaction of giving you a compliment, and allow yourself to enjoy the praise and recognition.

Second, if you find yourself discounting the positives and making "Yes, but..." statements, write them down in your journal. Ask yourself whether these statements provide accurate, balanced views of the situation. (Hint: They probably don't.) Write a more accurate statement that acknowledges the positives. The more you practice doing this, the more automatic it will become. You'll start catching yourself in the moment and changing "Yes, but..." statements to "Yes, and..." statements that amplify the positives.

Ditch Double Standards

Double standards exist when rules or principles are applied in different ways to different people. If your teacher announced that students born in odd-numbered months would get 10 bonus points on the next exam, but students born in even-numbered months would not, there would be outrage! Double standards get our blood boiling because they're unfair. It's wrong to apply one set of rules to some people but a different set to others.

When you get caught in the perfectionism thinking trap, though, you engage in double standards. That's because you hold yourself to a higher set of standards than others. Consider Tommy's story.

> Tommy made high grades in the most challenging classes. If there was an advanced placement course available, Tommy took it and excelled in it. He was president of his school's environmental science club and secretary of the sports medicine club. He was also captain of the soccer team. From the outside, it seemed like Tommy had it all: model student, top athlete, and socially conscious teen. He seemed destined for greatness.
>
> But inside, Tommy was miserable. He was awake at 5:30 every morning and didn't get to bed until midnight because he was busy with homework and extracurricular activities. He couldn't accept a grade below an A. If he made a mistake in a soccer game, he replayed it over and over in his mind and told himself he could have avoided the mistake if he'd only trained harder. He felt exhausted, overwhelmed, and like a phony, because his life looked perfect from the outside but felt terrible on the inside. More and more, he thought about ending his life because he couldn't take the pressure.

Tommy was caught in the perfectionism trap. He applied standards to himself that were impossible to meet, and he beat himself up when he didn't meet them. The following beliefs, among others, drove Tommy's misery:

- I must be perfect in everything I do.

- I'm a failure if I don't get straight A's.

- My family will be disappointed in me if I'm not the best.

- Because I'm team captain, I can't make mistakes in soccer.

- I have to hold leadership positions in multiple clubs to get into the best college.

- People will think less of me if they know I struggle with stress and suicidal thoughts.

To push back on these beliefs and develop more accurate and healthy thoughts, Tommy could examine whether he applies the same standards to other people. He wrote down each belief in his journal and then asked himself it was true for someone else he knew. Here's what he realized:

- I must be perfect in everything I do.

  - My friends all make mistakes. I don't dislike them or think they're dumb because of it.

- I'm a failure if I don't get straight A's.

  - Most of my classmates get some B's and C's. They aren't failures.

- My family will be disappointed in me if I'm not the best.

  - My brother is terrible at sports and makes decent grades, but we love him and we're proud of him for who he is.

- Because I'm team captain, I can't make mistakes in soccer.

  - Adrian was team captain last year. He made a bunch of mistakes, and everyone still thought he was a great captain.

- I have to hold leadership positions in multiple clubs to get into the best college.

  - I have classmates who plan on going to good colleges, and they don't hold leadership positions.

- People will think less of me if they know I struggle with stress and suicidal thoughts.

  - Lots of my classmates talk about feeling stressed out. My friend Omar takes antidepressant medication, and my friend Sandi sees a therapist for help with an eating disorder. I don't think less of them.

It quickly became clear that Tommy held himself to much higher standards than he demanded of others. His unrealistic standards were contributing to his thoughts of suicide. To get out of the perfectionism trap, Tommy needed to ditch the double standards and generate more accurate and realistic thoughts, like these:

- Perfectionism tells me I must be perfect in everything I do.

  - Push back: It's impossible to be perfect. It's okay to make mistakes.

- Perfectionism tells me I'm a failure if I don't get straight A's.

  - Push back: That's ridiculous! Lots of successful people don't get straight A's.

- Perfectionism tells me my family will be disappointed in me if I'm not the best.

  - Push back: My family loves me and supports me no matter what.

- Perfectionism tells me because I'm team captain, I can't make mistakes in soccer.

  - Push back: Seriously? Every team captain in the history of every sport made mistakes.

- Perfectionism tells me I have to hold leadership positions in multiple clubs to get into the best college.

  - Push back: Not true. I know people who got into good colleges without being leaders.

- Perfectionism tells me people will think less of me if they know I struggle with stress and suicidal thoughts.

    - Push back: That's a double standard! Others will support me if I acknowledge my struggles. Besides, if someone does think less of me for that reason, I don't want to be around them.

It wasn't easy for Tommy to let go of perfectionism. He had to work hard to push back against the perfectionistic voice in his head. But with practice at catching the voice and pushing back, he began to cut back on extracurricular activities, get more sleep, and feel less pressured. His thoughts of suicide decreased as he realized how fun life could be when he allowed himself to be imperfect—and not try to do it all.

Think about the standards you hold for yourself. Do you identify areas where you get caught in the perfectionism trap? If so, write down the perfectionistic thoughts in your journal and then ask whether you hold other people to the same standard. If you identify double standards, come up with more realistic, accurate thoughts. When the perfectionistic voice gets loud, push back against it and ditch the double standards!

Remember, it's okay to be imperfect. Nobody's perfect, so why should you be the exception?

Talk Back!

Tommy pushed back on perfectionism by coming up with counter thoughts that contradicted what the perfectionistic voice said. Coming up with counter thoughts is a helpful strategy for pushing back on all thinking traps, not only perfectionism. This includes all-or-nothing thinking, the blame game, and beliefs about being trapped and pain being intolerable. Talking back to the negative voice in your head puts you in control of your thoughts. Being in control of your thoughts will also put you in control of your feelings and actions.

Whenever you hear the negative voice of thinking traps, stop and identify what it's telling you. Write it down in your journal so you know what you're up against. Then ask yourself these ten questions:

1. What evidence supports this thought?

2. What evidence doesn't support this thought?

3. Are there other possible explanations?

4. Are there other ways to think about this situation?

5. What would I say to a friend who had this thought?

6. What's the worst that could happen?

7. Is this extreme thinking? Is there a more accurate middle ground?

8. Am I making assumptions or jumping to conclusions?

9. What positive things might I be overlooking?

10. Would I apply the same standard to others?

Asking yourself these questions will help you obtain new information and consider other perspectives, which will lead to changes in the way you think. After asking yourself these questions, come up with a counter thought that pushes back on the negative voice.

To strengthen your counter thought skills, practice talking back to the negative thoughts listed here. These are common negative thoughts that can bring you down and trigger thoughts of suicide. We've talked back to the first one. Have some fun talking back to the rest as you practice generating counter thoughts! Write down your counter thoughts in your journal so you can refer back to them in the future.

Negative Voice   The only way to escape my pain is to kill myself.

Talk Back!   That's not true! There are several things I can do right now to manage my painful feelings, including talking to my friend Ashley, doing yoga, and savoring pleasant memories.

Negative Voice   Things will never get better.   **Talk Back!**

Negative Voice   I'm a drain on others.   **Talk Back!**

Negative Voice   People don't like me.   **Talk Back!**

Negative Voice   There's something wrong with me.   **Talk Back!**

Negative Voice   There's no point in living.   **Talk Back!**

Negative Voice   There's never anything to do.   **Talk Back!**

Negative Voice   I'm going to fail.   **Talk Back!**

Negative Voice   I can't handle this.   **Talk Back!**

Negative Voice   I have no control over my life.   **Talk Back!**

Negative Voice   Good things never happen to me.   **Talk Back!**

Negative Voice   Life is terrible.   **Talk Back!**

Now that you're finding *your* voice and generating ideas for talking back to the negative voice, watch for negative thoughts in the coming week. Write them down when they happen, ask yourself the ten questions, and generate counter thoughts to talk back to them. Say the counter thoughts aloud multiple times. Don't let the negative voice win the argument! As you talk back to the negative voice, your outlook on life will become more flexible and balanced, allowing you to enjoy the positives here and now and be more hopeful about your future.

WHEN NEGATIVE THOUGHTS ARE ACCURATE

As you've seen in this chapter, there are many ways the negative voice in your head can ensnare you in thinking traps. In most situations, the negative voice is simply wrong and tries to make you believe things are much worse than they really are. But sometimes bad things happen, and sometimes negative thoughts accurately reflect the reality of bad situations. You'll fail sometimes. People will hurt you sometimes. Illnesses, accidents, and natural disasters will happen.

Sometimes you'll question the negative voice and finds it's accurate. What can you do then? In chapter 5, you will learn to identify what you can and can't control. This includes recognizing and accepting that some things in life are beyond your control, and then focusing your efforts and energy on how you respond to what you *can* control! Practice strategies to manage your emotions and reduce stress. Lean into your support network. And keep questioning the negative voice to make sure it doesn't pull you into a trap. When life gets tough, the negative voice will get loud to try to convince you things will never get better and there's nothing you can do. Those are traps! Identify them, question them, and talk back.

MOVING FORWARD

In this chapter, you've learned to identify the negative voice in your head. You've learned about common thinking traps the negative voice uses to ensnare you and promote thoughts of suicide. Most important, you've learned tips for pushing back against the negative voice to develop more flexible, accurate, and healthy ways of thinking about yourself, the world, and your future.

Keep a log of your thoughts and counter thoughts to make sure you, not the negative voice, stay in control of your thoughts, feelings, and actions. Remember to focus daily on the positives, especially the small things that often get overlooked. Appreciate your good qualities, and recognize what makes each day worth living!

In the next chapter, you'll learn to identify the things that stress you out, and you'll gain valuable strategies for coping with stress.

CHAPTER 5

Identifying and Managing Stress

Stress is a word that can make us uneasy—just saying it can make you feel tense! But it doesn't have to be that way. To start becoming more comfortable with the idea of stress, let's break down what it is.

Stress is a feeling of pressure or strain in response to circumstances in your life. You experience stress when you think you're unable to meet a demand or challenge. For example, a pop quiz produces stress because you think you're not adequately prepared. If the quiz turns out to be easy, your stress quickly disappears because you met the challenge!

To understand and manage stress, we need to distinguish it from *stressors*. Stressors are the external events or circumstances that place demands on you, like pop quizzes. Stress is what you experience internally, the feeling of pressure or strain you get in response to stressors. This distinction matters because you can improve the quality of your life by reducing external stressors in your life, managing your internal experiences of stress, or both.

Many teens think about stress as acute, meaning it comes up and spikes suddenly in response to a specific event. For example, you tense up suddenly when you receive a bad grade on an important test, or learn your grandparent had a heart attack, or your romantic partner breaks up with you. Acute stress is short-lived but intense.

Stress can also be chronic, hanging around in response to ongoing circumstances. For example, you may feel tense much of the time if you live in an unsafe neighborhood, or someone close to you suffers from chronic health problems, or your parents argue regularly. Chronic stress isn't as intense as acute stress, but it can make you feel tense and upset for longer.

Both acute and chronic stress can affect your physical and mental well-being. They also can trigger thoughts of suicide. Teens who experience higher levels of acute and chronic stress are more likely to think about suicide, and most teens who attempt suicide report experiencing acute stress, or stressful life events, in the preceding days. Any type of stress can trigger thoughts of suicide because it creates discomfort and tension, but some types of stress are especially likely to trigger thoughts of suicide in teens: romantic relationship problems, conflict with parents, and legal or disciplinary problems.

In this chapter, you'll learn four strategies for managing your stress. First, let's look at the stressful experiences of other teens.

Tuesday began like any other day for Shae, but things took a turn for the worse when they got on the bus. As Shae walked down the aisle, half-asleep, to find a seat, the most annoying jerk in tenth grade, Jason, stuck out his leg and tripped them. Jason sarcastically said, "Oops, my bad," while laughing with his friends. Shae ignored him—they didn't need the drama this early in the morning. Shae had almost forgotten about the bus incident by lunch, but then Jason struck again. As they walked toward a table with a tray full of food, Jason bumped into them on purpose, resulting in Shae tumbling over directly onto a plate of spaghetti. That was it—Shae snapped! They threw the tray at Jason and tackled him. Shae could hear classmates yelling as they wrestled on the lunchroom floor. Suddenly, an immense pressure hit the middle of Shae's back as a security guard place his knee—and entire weight—on them. Shae felt handcuffs dig tightly into their wrists as the security guard lifted them up and pushed them toward the exit. After Shae waited for what felt like an eternity in spaghetti-covered clothes and painfully tight handcuffs, the principal showed up and suspended Shae from school for a week! The principal had no interest in hearing Shae's side of the story. Shae had never gotten in trouble at school before. Now they would miss a whole week of school, including two big tests later this week. As this reality set in, Shae's thoughts of suicide started coming back.

Jaylin's parents are *always* arguing. Peace and quiet don't exist when they are both at home. Sometimes they bicker about petty stuff like who's washing the dishes or taking Jaylin to art class. Other times it escalates to yelling and threats to leave home. Jaylin hates hearing them fight, especially when their fights involve him and his younger sister. He doesn't know how much longer he can stand it. He's thought about running away from home, but he doesn't leave because he feels like his sister needs him.

Sammie has been dating Sebastian for five months. At first, she felt special with all the attention he gave her, like how he always waited for her after class and texted her sweet messages when they weren't together. But now he's getting possessive. If she doesn't arrive at the moment he expects, he calls and asks where she is. If she talks to friends, he seems irritable and wants to know what they're talking about. He gets really mad when she talks to her male friends. Sammie has started to avoid her friends because she doesn't want to create conflict with Sebastian. One day Sammie's friend Julian caught up to her in the hall and walked her to her next class. During class, Sammie got a text from Sebastian saying he needed to see her NOW. Sammie told the teacher she needed to go to the restroom and then left class to find Sebastian by her locker. He was so angry that his hands were shaking. He asked her why she was talking to Julian if she cared about him. Sammie told Sebastian he was making her uncomfortable and she was going back to class. As she tried to walk away, Sebastian grabbed her arm and pushed her against the locker. He told her never to talk to Julian again and said she would be sorry if she did. Sammie felt scared. She was afraid to talk to anyone about Sebastian's threats and started to think about ending her life as a way to escape the stressful situation.

Even though their circumstances differed, Shae, Jaylin, and Sammie all experienced stress. Shae experienced acute stress—things were generally going okay but then went off the rails in a hurry when Jason bullied them. Jaylin's stress was different. There wasn't a single event that created tension and problems for him. Instead, Jaylin experienced a chronically stressful home environment because his parents were constantly fighting. He felt on edge at home even when he wasn't directly involved in the conflict. Sammie experienced a double whammy—both chronic and acute stress. Sammie was chronically tense because of Sebastian's ongoing jealous behavior; then she experienced a specific stressful event on top of it when he became physically aggressive and threatened her.

In the rest of this chapter, you'll learn strategies to manage stress, and you'll see how these strategies can be applied to the difficult situations faced by Shae, Jaylin, and Sammie. You'll also focus on how you can apply the strategies to manage stress in your life.

IDENTIFY YOUR STRESS

Before you can manage stress, you must identify it. It's especially important to identify stress that triggers thoughts of suicide, because that's the stress you'll need to manage to stay safe and build a better, more hope-filled future.

We're going to ask you to reflect on stressors you have experienced recently. Reflecting on stressors can be, well, stressful! It can bring up painful memories and feelings. If you feel stressed or upset as you work through this chapter, take a break to soothe yourself. Use the strategies from chapter 3 that you found most helpful in managing your feelings, like breathing, acceptance, or adopting a different perspective. If thinking about stressors brings up suicidal thoughts, use the plan you developed in chapter 2 to stay safe. If you need to reach out to someone for help, do it!

Although thinking about bad things that have happened can be unpleasant, it's a necessary step on the path to learning how to manage your stress. That's because it provides helpful information about where you need to apply the strategies we'll cover later in this chapter.

You'll need your journal for this section. Look through the list of examples of stressors that teens commonly experience, and identify any that you have experienced in the last few months. It doesn't matter when the stressors happened; if they seem relevant to you, write them down. Also write down other stressors you've experienced that aren't listed here. Allow space to later add information after each one.

- Did poorly on a test or major assignment
- Repeated a grade
- Too much homework to complete
- Changed schools
- Dropped out of school
- Got in trouble with a teacher or principal
- Got suspended from school
- Pressure to perform well
- Problems with a peer at school
- Death of pet
- Death of someone close to you
- Serious illness or injury of someone close to you
- Serious illness or injury
- Family member lost a job
- Had to care for siblings
- Family struggled to pay the bills
- Not enough money to pay for something you needed
- No transportation to get to where you needed to go
- Eviction
- Had to take on extra hours at work

- Too many responsibilities to manage
- Parents separated or divorced
- Parents seriously argued
- Serious argument with family member
- Serious argument with friend
- Serious argument with romantic partner
- Got into a physical fight
- Friendship ended
- Romantic relationship ended
- Romantic partner cheated on you
- Not enough friends
- Lack of a desired romantic partner
- Unplanned pregnancy
- Parents disappointed in you
- Coach or teacher disappointed in you
- Friend disappointed in you
- Criticized behind your back
- Discrimination for your race or ethnicity
- Discrimination for your sexual or gender orientation
- Someone gossiped or lied about you behind your back
- Someone made fun of you
- Arrested
- Speeding ticket/traffic citation
- Car accident
- Moved to a new place
- Theft
- Assaulted by someone
- Natural disaster

Clearly stress can happen in different areas of life. Common areas where teens experience stress include school, health, finances, family relationships, peer relationships, romantic relationships, legal troubles, and transitions like changing schools. Identifying the areas where you commonly experience stress helps you know where to apply the strategies we'll cover here, including steps you can take to reduce the frequency of stressors.

Now look through the list of stressors you wrote in your journal. Beside each, write down the following:

- Number of times it happened in the last several months, as best you recall

- The area(s) in which it happened (for example, school)

- How much it bothered you on a scale from 1 to 10, with 1 meaning it didn't bother you at all and 10 meaning it bothered you very, very much

For an example, look at this table of hypothetical common stressors (we'll explain the stars soon):

What happened?	# of times in last few months	Area	How much it bothered me
Peers made fun of my weight*	4	Peer relationships	8
Got a bad grade in math	2	School	4
Didn't have enough money to go out	1	Financial	5
Argued with parents about my choice of friends	3	Family relationships	7
Peer said something bad about me behind my back	1	Peer relationships	9
Wanted to go to the dance but didn't have anyone to go with	1	Romantic relationships	7
Didn't have friends to hang out with*	>10	Peer relationships	6

Now that you have your list of stressors, their frequency, the areas in which they happened, and how much they bothered you, can you identify patterns or themes? Do you tend to experience stress in one or two areas more than in others? In the table, the most common stressors involved peer relationships and the second most common involved family relationships. That's pretty typical for teens.

Do certain types or areas of stress consistently upset you more than others? In the table, stressors in peer relationships were more upsetting than stressors in other areas. What area(s) upset you most?

Is your stress mostly acute (specific events), chronic (ongoing challenges), or a mix of both? The table includes mostly acute stressors, but not having friends to hang out with was a chronic source of stress.

As you reflect on the stressors you experienced, note which, if any, triggered thoughts of hurting yourself or ending your life. Stress in some areas tends to push our buttons more than others, meaning it bothers us deeply when problems happen in those areas. If you identify stressors that triggered suicidal thoughts, put a star beside them on your list. In the example list, being made fun of about weight and not having friends triggered thoughts of suicide, as indicated by the star beside them. It's important to flag stressors that trigger thoughts of suicide, because those are the stressors you'll need to manage to stay safe.

Sometimes it's hard to remember stressors that happened in the past and how much it bothered you at the time. If you found it hard to come up with a list of stressors, in the next week keep a log of stressors you experience, making sure to identify the areas in which they occur and how much they bother you. As you monitor your stressors, you'll start to identify patterns and themes that can help you understand when to use the following strategies. If you don't identify patterns or themes yet, that's okay—you can still apply the strategies!

STRATEGY #1: SIDESTEP YOUR STRESSORS

The first strategy for managing your stress is to reduce the number of stressors you experience. Recall that stress is your internal experience in response to external stressors. If the number of external stressors you experience decreases, it naturally follows that your stress will decrease, too!

Sounds too easy, right? If you could just stop stressful things from happening, you would have already done it. Some stressors are out of your control—we'll discuss that more under Strategy #4. But other stressors are predictable, and you can make changes to prevent some of them from happening, or at least make them happen less often. So, while it isn't easy to reduce stressors, it is possible, and you can do it!

There is no single way to reduce stressors, but naming this explicitly as a goal will help. It will keep you in tune with stressors occurring in your life and focused on possible ways to prevent them from occurring. Here's how:

First, review the list of stressors you wrote in your journal. Identify the most frequently occurring stressor in your life recently and the area in which it occurred. Circle it. If multiple stressors occurred with the same frequency, select the one that bothered you the most.

Next, brainstorm things you could do to try to prevent that stressor from happening. Write down ideas in your journal. There is no one-size-fits-all solution that can prevent all stressors from happening—every solution has to be tailored to the stressor. That said, some general tips apply to prevent stressors that fall within specific areas, as you'll see.

School Problems

If your stressor is in the area of school problems—for example, you did poorly on important tests or didn't finish assignments—you can use time management and study skills to prevent this from happening as frequently. Keep an academic planner and record homework and upcoming quizzes or tests. Create a study plan, designating blocks of time each day to complete assignments or study for tests. Then stick to it! Identify a quiet place with minimal distractions to study or complete assignments. Smartphones, social media, and online videos are especially distracting, so plan to turn off your phone or put it out of reach during your designated study time. Finally, reward yourself for achieving your study goals! If you set a goal to study or do homework for one hour without interruption, when the hour's up reward yourself by doing something fun for fifteen minutes, such as watching online videos, checking social media, or taking a short walk. After your rewarding break, return to your studies.

Search the internet or talk to your teachers for other ideas on how to manage your study time and implement study skills. By creating a study plan and sticking to it, you'll reduce your academic stressors and improve your academic performance! It may seem like a small step, but remember that any decrease in stressors, even small, will translate to less stress in your life, and less stress can result in fewer thoughts of suicide.

Relationship Problems

If you selected a stressor that involves relationships with other people, there are a few options you can try based on the nature of the relationship stressor. For example, if it primarily involves conflict, like arguments with a parent, you can walk away from heated situations before a disagreement escalates to a highly stressful level. Remember the emotion management strategy of buying time from chapter 3. When you notice a conversation starting to shift toward hot-button issues that result in heated arguments, hit the pause button, change the subject, or say you need to step away from the conversation. This will short-circuit an argument or fight before it starts, preventing the stressor from occurring. Of course, sometimes the other person might not let it go or might continue to bring up the subject the next time you see them, and sometimes you'll need to have difficult conversations to resolve differences, so this tip won't always prevent conflict. But you can use it to reduce conflict some of the time, and having fewer conflicts (stressors) means less stress overall!

If your relationship stressor primarily involves being overlooked, neglected, or treated unkindly by others, you can reduce the frequency of the stressor by practicing assertiveness. Assertiveness means being honest, confident, and direct in saying what you want to say. It's speaking up for yourself while respecting others.

Some people struggle to understand the difference between being assertive and being aggressive. Like assertiveness, aggressiveness involves being direct and speaking up for yourself. The difference is that aggressiveness isn't respectful of others; it violates others' rights or hurts them to achieve what you want. Assertiveness is also different from passivity. Passivity means accepting whatever happens without resisting or speaking up for yourself. Passivity avoids conflict, which may seem like a way to reduce stress. The problem with passivity is, you end up not getting what you want in situations. It allows others to push you around and take advantage of you, so you feel disappointed, upset, and resentful.

To illustrate the differences between assertiveness, aggressiveness, and passiveness, consider this situation: You feel uncomfortable when a friend at school asks to copy your math homework, but you worry the friend will get mad if you tell her no. How do you respond?

- *Assertive response:* "No. I worked hard on that assignment, and I don't feel comfortable being a part of cheating."

- *Aggressive response:* "Forget you! It's not my fault you're too lazy to do your work."

- *Passive response:* "Well…okay."

See the differences? Assertive responses reduce stressors because they set boundaries while respecting others. Setting boundaries, saying no, and not taking on too much are valuable skills to sidestep stressors and keep you from feeling overwhelmed. Assertive responses also ensure that you get noticed and treated with respect. By contrast, aggressive responses often result in conflict, and passive responses get your rights trampled. Of course, sometimes people won't like it when you respond assertively. That might generate conflict in the short term, but as you practice being assertive consistently, others will learn to respect your boundaries.

Finally, if you notice that your relationship stressors routinely involve a specific person or persons, consider ways to reduce the amount of time you spend with them. Some people tend to create stress and tension wherever they go. Maybe they stir up trouble by gossiping or pitting people against each other, maybe they drag you into their problems, or maybe you just don't click with them on a personal level. Whatever the reason, spending time with someone who generates stress is going to make you feel tense, even if it's someone you like.

To reduce your stressors, find ways to create space and distance from this person. Creating space can be challenging in some cases, like when it's a family member you live with. But even in those cases, if you identify when and where conflict most frequently occurs, you can take action to try to prevent it. For example, if arguments with your parent tend to happen at night when you're both tired from a long day at work and school, consider going to different rooms at night to reduce the opportunities for sparks to fly. You'll learn more about how to sidestep stressful relationships in chapter 6.

After you've tried out some approaches to reducing one stressor, pick another stressor from your list and identify possible ways to reduce it, too. While it's unrealistic to expect to eliminate all stressors, when you identify stressors and develop ways to reduce the chances of them happening, you'll find yourself feeling less stressed, and that will translate into fewer thoughts of suicide.

STRATEGY #2: INCREASE YOUR MOOD BOOSTERS

Strategy #1 was about decreasing the frequency of negative events. Strategy #2 is about increasing the frequency of positive events. This is a helpful strategy to manage stress for at least two reasons. One, the more you experience positive events, the less time and opportunity you have to experience negative events. There are twenty-four hours in a day, about sixteen of which you're awake. The more time you spend in positive activities, the less time you'll spend caught up in negative events. Two, positive events shift your thoughts and feelings in a positive, pleasant direction. You can think of positive events as mood boosters that result in your feeling better and being less likely to have thoughts of suicide.

When stressors happen, people often experience negative feelings, direct their attention to their negative feelings and the troubling thing that happened, and stop doing things they used to enjoy doing. Then they get stuck in a downward spiral of negative thoughts and feelings that can descend into thoughts of suicide. To pull out of that spiral, engage in positive activities that redirect your thoughts and attention to pleasant things and bring about positive feelings like happiness, interest, and enjoyment (Curry et al., 2005).

It's a simple concept: if you do things you enjoy, you will experience joy. But sometimes simple concepts are hard to put into practice. Let's begin by taking inventory. Earlier in this chapter, you listed recent stressors you'd experienced. Now, in your journal, write down recent positive activities you've enjoyed. To help you identify what these might include, turn back to chapter 2, where we listed fun coping activities. If any apply, write those down. That list is definitely not exhaustive, so be sure to write down other positive or fun activities you've done that aren't shown there.

Now look at the list of positive activities that you wrote in your journal. Beside each activity, write down the following:

- Number of times you did it in the last month, as best as you can remember.

- How much you enjoy the activity, on a scale from 1 to 10, with 1 meaning you don't enjoy it at all, 5 meaning you find it moderately pleasurable or engaging, and 10 meaning you absolutely love doing it! Any activity that you rate higher than 5 is a mood booster.

To illustrate what it could look like, here's a hypothetical example of a mood boosters list:

Positive Event	# of times in last month	How much I enjoyed it
Baked cookies*	2	6
Played a game online with others*	8	7
Wrote poetry	1	3
Solved a puzzle	3	5
Hung out with friends*	1	7
Went to movies*	1	8
Went to a restaurant	4	4

Reflect on your list. What activities do you enjoy most, and how often have you done them in the last month? In the hypothetical example, the most frequent activity was playing games online with others, and it was pretty fun—a rating of 7! Going to the movies was the most enjoyable activity; writing poetry and going to restaurants were okay but not a blast. Other mood boosters in the hypothetical list include baking cookies and hanging out with friends. We put a star beside those activities because they earned a fun rating higher than 5. Identify activities on your list with a fun rating higher than 5 and put a star beside them. Those are good mood boosters—the types of activities you can do more frequently to improve your mood and reduce stress.

Are there other activities you enjoy but didn't do last month? If so, write them down in your journal. If you had trouble coming up with activities, or if none of your activities are mood boosters, write down a few activities you might like to try or activities that you enjoyed doing in the past. Also, keep a log of your activities in the coming week, making sure to rate how much you enjoy them.

Now let's turn to increasing your mood boosters. Select the top three mood boosters from your list, or if you don't have three, select activities you would like to try. Make sure the activities you select are things you have control over and will be able to do in the next week. For example, "going to Disney World" probably isn't something you have control over, but "drawing a picture," "calling a friend," or "going for a run" are activities you can do in any space of free time.

Identify a day, time, and place you can engage in each of the three mood boosters at least once this week. In your journal, write down each mood booster, as well as when and where you'll do it—you're more likely to follow through with a plan if you write it down! Also, consider setting a reminder in your phone so you don't forget.

After you complete a mood booster, write down how much you enjoyed it. If your rating is higher than 5, that's great! Keep doing it! If your rating is 5 or below, that's okay, but it suggests you should try another activity that will be more effective at boosting your mood. If you forget to do an activity or you can't do an activity on your list, that's okay, too. Select a different activity that you have more control over, and give that a try instead.

Continue scheduling mood-boosting activities every week, aiming to increase the number of positive activities you engage in. As you do so, you'll find that your mood becomes more consistently positive and you feel less stressed. You'll probably also find that thoughts of suicide arise less frequently.

STRATEGY #3: BECOME A PROBLEM SOLVER

Our third strategy for managing stress is problem-solving. Sidestepping stressors and boosting your mood can help you feel better, but inevitably you'll face stressors and problems in life—we all do—so you need to have ways to solve them. It's common for teens to experience distress and thoughts of suicide when problems happen. Problem-solving can be a useful skill to prevent thoughts of suicide that arise following small hassles or big challenges. In fact, teens who have learned problem-solving skills are less likely to think about suicide following stressful events than teens who don't yet know how to break down and solve problems (Grover, Green, Pettit, Garza, Monteith, & Venta, 2009). That's because when you don't know how to solve a problem, it can make you feel overwhelmed and hopeless. You might say to yourself that if there's nothing you can do about something bad in your life, maybe the only way out is to kill yourself. That's a trap, so don't get caught in it!

When you learn how to solve problems, you'll avoid the trap and feel more in control of your life, confident when facing challenges, and hopeful about your future. So how do you become a problem solver?

1. Identify the problem and write it down in your journal.

2. Create a list of all possible solutions to the problem. Be creative! List every option you can think of to solve the problem, even if it doesn't seem like something you would ever do, because sometimes what seems like a bad idea at first actually turns out to be helpful. By listing all possible solutions, you give yourself more options for dealing with a

problem. If you find it difficult to come up with possible solutions, try the strategy of adopting a different perspective that you learned in chapter 3: imagine someone else was facing this problem. What might you tell them to try as possible solutions?

3. Evaluate each of the possible solutions you listed. Keep in mind there will never be a *perfect* solution to any problem, but there usually are good solutions for whatever problem you face. Weigh the pros and cons of each, and try to envision the likely outcome. Then rank order the solutions, with 1 for the best, 2 for second best, and so on.

4. Now look at your #1 choice and give it a try.

5. Evaluate whether your action solved the problem. If yes, great! That's success! If no, that's okay. Just as there are no perfect solutions to any problem, there are no guarantees the solution you select will have the intended outcome. When that happens, go back to your list of possible solutions and repeat step 4 with your second choice. Then evaluate whether it worked. Keep going until you find an acceptable solution to your problem. If none of the solutions solved the problem, consider asking a trusted friend or adult for help generating solutions. Sometimes an outside perspective can help when you get stuck on a difficult problem.

Like most things, problem-solving takes practice. The more you use it, even for easy-to-solve problems, the more natural it will feel and the better you'll get at coming up with effective solutions quickly. That's a valuable skill, because you'll face problems big and small in life. Having a strategy to handle those problems can make a big difference between feeling stuck and hopeless or empowered and optimistic!

STRATEGY #4: IDENTIFY WHAT YOU CAN AND CAN'T CONTROL

Decreasing stressors, increasing mood boosters, and problem-solving are effective ways to manage stress. But we've got to be realistic. Some things are outside your control. The following list helps to illustrate this reality. In your journal, make two columns labeled "Controllable" and "Uncontrollable." Place each of these items in the appropriate column.

What other people say	Politics
What other people do	War and conflict between countries
How other people treat you	The economy
What other people think about you	Your sleep schedule
What happened in the past	What you eat and drink
Who your family members are	Your breathing
How healthy or sick other people are	Your self-care
What you say	How you respond to your feelings
What you do	What you watch
How you treat other people	What you listen to
The weather	Crime

After classifying these items as either controllable or uncontrollable, do you pick up on a theme? Here it is: you can control only your own actions. You have no control over many things in life, including many things that happen to you.

You can't stop bad things from happening any more than you can stop the wind from blowing. You can't make other people think, feel, or act a certain way. You can't change the past. The more you try to control things outside of your control, the more frustrated, upset, and hopeless you'll feel. You might even think a life that feels so out of control isn't worth living, but that's another trap! Recognizing what you can and can't control, and learning to let go of trying to control what you can't, can feel like a heavy burden being lifted off of you.

Look back at the list of stressors you wrote down in your journal earlier in this chapter. Place the letter C beside stressors you can control and the letter U beside stressors you can't control. If a stressor is partially but not completely under your control, put C/U beside it. That would be the case when you can do things to influence whether something does or doesn't happen, but you can't fully control the outcome. Here's how it would look for the hypothetical list of stressors we presented earlier in the chapter:

What happened?	Controllable or Uncontrollable?
Peers made fun of my weight	U–Can't control peers' actions
Got a bad grade in math	C–Can control doing my homework
Didn't have enough money to go out	C/U–Not old enough to have a job, but could try to get paid for babysitting or doing chores
Argued with parents about my choice of friends	C–Can be assertive without losing my cool
Peer said something bad about me behind my back	U–Can't control what peers say or do
Wanted to go to the dance but didn't have anyone to go with	C/U–Could have asked someone to the dance but can't control how they respond
Didn't have friends to hang out with	C/U–Could invite people to hang out, but can't control how they respond

As you can see from the hypothetical examples, some stressors are definitely out of your control, some are definitely under your control, and others are mixed. Mixed stressors means you can take action to reduce the chances of the stressor happening, but you can't control how other people respond.

Turn back to your list of stressors. Ask yourself, *What can I control in this situation?* Identify what you can and can't control, and then focus your efforts and energy on the things you can control: your actions and responses in situations. Look for ways to reduce the occurrence of stressors and increase mood-boosting activities. Use problem-solving to identify, try out, and evaluate solutions. For mixed stressors that are partly but not completely under your control, use the same strategies to identify ways to address the parts you can control.

When you can't control what happens externally, focus your efforts on what's happening inside you and how you respond to situations. Remember the strategies for thoughtful responding in chapter 3, such as belly breathing and accepting feelings. Specifically, you can use breathing as a relaxation strategy if you feel stressed about a situation you can't control. You can practice acceptance of your feelings and also accept that you don't have the power to change the situation. That doesn't mean you give up, become hopeless, or allow yourself to remain in bad situations when you have the power to do something about it. Instead, it's a realistic acknowledgment of our limitations as humans and a powerful statement that you're in control of your actions regardless of what happens to you. Accepting what you can't control allows you to focus your efforts and energy on what you *can* control. To repeat, how you respond *is* under your control and can make a big difference in how you think and feel!

For example, if you remember something hurtful you said to a family member in the past, acknowledge that you can't change what already happened; instead, think about how you can control how you act toward that family member in the future. If you find yourself starting to worry whether somebody likes you, acknowledge that you can't control this; then think about how you can control how you act around that person and what you say to them. If someone at school says mean things about you, acknowledge that you can't control what they say, and then focus on how you can control how you respond (assertively!) and with whom you choose to spend your time.

Sadly, there's no magic wand we can wave to prevent all bad things from happening or the pain they cause. By understanding what is and isn't under your control, though, you'll be able to be steer your life experiences in positive, less stressful directions. You'll also learn to let go of things that cause you stress and frustration. The result will be a calmer life with less stress to trigger thoughts of suicide.

APPLICATION

Let's return to Shae, Jaylin, and Sammie and see how you might apply these four strategies to their stressful situations.

> Following their fight in school, Shae was in a tough spot. Shae was suspended from school and was going to miss two big tests. What strategies could they use to manage their stress? A good starting place would be to take inventory of what they can and can't control. As much as they might want to, they can't go back and change what Jason did to them or how Shae reacted in the cafeteria. The past is in the past. Shae also can't control the fact that they are suspended now. What they can control is how they respond to this situation and what steps they take to minimize the damage. This recognition of what they can and can't control helped Shae avoid falling into the trap of repeatedly playing the negative events over in their mind and feeling hopeless about their situation. It also empowered them to use a second strategy: problem-solving.

Shae identified one important problem and wrote it down: "I need to take two tests, but I won't be in school." Shae then spent time thinking about possible solutions and wrote them down:

- Sneak into class secretly when the teachers give the tests.

- Drop out of school.

- Just don't take the tests at all.

- Email my teachers and ask if I can take the tests at home or online.

- Email the teachers and ask if I can make up the tests after my suspension is over.

After weighing the pros and cons of each possible solution, Shae ranked emailing their teachers to ask if they could take the tests at home or online as the best option. This would allow them to stay on track in their schoolwork. Plus, even though Shae was very disappointed about being suspended, the silver lining was that it would give them more time to study for the tests.

Shae wrote nice, respectful emails to their teachers and asked a friend to review them. After receiving their friend's approval, Shae sent the emails. One teacher replied the same day, the other the following day. Both said they wished they could allow Shae to take the tests at home, but school policy prevented them from administering tests to students during their suspension. The teachers offered to let Shae take the tests as soon as the suspension ended. Even though that wasn't Shae's top choice solution, they felt relieved knowing they wouldn't get a zero or fall behind on important tests.

Jaylin's home life was chronically stressful because his parents fought with each other so much. What could he do to manage this stress? Like Shae, Jaylin started by evaluating what he could and couldn't control. He couldn't control what his parents did. He had tried to stop their fighting in the past, but it just got him pulled into the conflict. He also couldn't change who his family members were or where he lived. He could, however, control some of his exposure to the stressors.

Jaylin realized he could sidestep some stressors by getting out of the house when his parents fought. For example, when his parents' fights grew intense, he could take his little sister outside to play or shoot basketball, or he could walk to the park at the end of his street. If it was too late to go outside or the weather was too cold or wet, he could go to another room in the house, put his earbuds in, and listen to music so he wouldn't hear them arguing. This wouldn't stop his parents from fighting, of course, but he would feel less stressed because he wasn't so exposed to it.

Jaylin also used mood boosters as a strategy to manage stress. He identified three activities he enjoyed but hadn't done recently: drawing portraits, playing video games with friends, and attending art club meetings at his school. He found the meeting schedule for the art club and added the meetings to his phone calendar. He also scheduled weekly times to draw portraits for at least two hours and invited two friends to play his favorite game, League of Legends, for an hour.

Although Jaylin couldn't resolve the problems between his parents, he found that he was less stressed and in a better mood after taking these steps. He also felt more hopeful about his future because he realized he could work around difficult situations and create a happier, less stressful life for himself.

Sammie was in a chronically stressful relationship and experienced aggression and threats from her boyfriend, Sebastian. What strategies could she use to manage her stress? Sammie decided the first thing she needed to do was reduce her stressors. She realized that much of her stress revolved around one person: Sebastian. To decrease the stress in her life, she needed space and distance from him. But how could she do that? She was afraid of how would he react if she broke up with him or ghosted him.

Sammie decided to ask for help. She worried that her parents would overreact and do something crazy if they found out Sebastian had threatened her, so she reached out to Ms. Gonzalez, her school counselor. Sammie trusted that Ms. Gonzalez could help her figure out solutions without overreacting. In their scheduled meeting, she felt scared but explained her situation anyway and asked if Ms. Gonzalez could help her problem solve. Just talking about her situation with someone caring like Ms. Gonzalez provided a huge sense of relief! Ms. Gonzalez helped Sammie think through several possible solutions and decide on one. Sammie would be assertive with Sebastian, telling him directly that she liked him but was made uncomfortable by his jealous behavior, and she would end their relationship if he continued acting that way. She role-played what she would say and how she would say it with Ms. Gonzalez. She also made a plan to tell Sebastian over the phone while she was in the room with Ms. Gonzalez, because that would ensure her safety at the moment.

Sammie felt super nervous when she called Sebastian. She took several deep breaths, reminded herself of what she planned to say, and told herself that this was important to do for her well-being. The call wasn't perfect, but Sebastian responded better than Sammie had expected. He apologized, said he didn't want to hurt or threaten her, and committed to not act that way again. Sammie wasn't sure whether Sebastian would follow through on his commitment, but she felt empowered having told him directly how she felt and having set a firm boundary. Instead of feeling afraid and powerless, she felt confident that she could handle issues that arise in the future. She also learned that ending her life wasn't the only solution to her problem.

Now that you've seen how these stress-management strategies were applied by Shae, Jaylin, and Sammie, think about how you might apply them to situations you're facing now. It won't always be easy, and it's even possible your stress levels may go up a little when you first try to use these strategies. That's normal—after all, they are new to you. But keep at it! If you're intentional in using these strategies, you'll find that your stress levels go down, your happiness goes up, and thoughts of suicide become less frequent.

MOVING FORWARD

In this chapter, you've learned strategies to manage stress and seen how those strategies can be applied to examples of other teens who found themselves in stressful circumstances. You've learned to distinguish stress from stressors and to manage stress by reducing the number of negative events in your life and increasing mood boosters, or positive activities. Most of all, you've learned the value of identifying what you can and can't control in life. You've also picked up problem-solving as a helpful strategy when problems can't be avoided.

Remember to monitor your stressors and mood boosters regularly and to practice these strategies for managing your stress. With regular practice, these strategies will begin to feel automatic and will enable you to face situations with confidence, knowing you can handle what life throws at you.

In the next chapter, you'll explore how to build and strengthen your relationships—and how to get out of harmful relationships.

CHAPTER 6

Building Relationships

Birthday parties, holidays, graduations, weddings, and other family gatherings—so many of the major events in our lives are celebrated or shared with others. The same is true in our day-to-day lives. School sports, dances, lunch room conversations, and classroom discussions. You spend an enormous portion of your life in the presence of other people. It's no wonder, then, that connecting with others is critical to your health and happiness. The need for relationships—family, friends, partners, acquaintances, and more—is part of what makes us human.

Relationships are important! Relationships give us space to feel secure, express ourselves, and connect with others. Relationships give us people to laugh and cry with. Relationships also allow us to be part of something bigger than ourselves and connect with the world around us. But *because* relationships are so important, when our need to belong is not met, it can be particularly painful. Isolation, loneliness, rejection, and loss are some of the most painful emotions we can experience. (As of this writing, we're entering the third year of pandemic restrictions with no clear end in sight. Trying to build and maintain relationships has been challenging for everyone during the pandemic, but it has been particularly difficult for teens. If you feel like your relationships have struggled during this time, you are not alone!) And while everyone feels lonely or rejected *sometimes*, feeling that way much or all of the time can lead to depression, hopelessness, and thoughts of suicide.

Building strong, healthy relationships and creating connections with others makes life more enjoyable, keeps you balanced and supported, and can help protect you from suicidal thoughts. In chapter 2, you tapped into your existing relationships when developing your safety plan. That's because connecting with others is an important part of meeting your psychological needs. Just as you need food, water, and shelter to keep yourself physically healthy, you need relationships to keep yourself mentally healthy. In this chapter you'll focus on how to build up your relationships and social support network, strengthen the relationships you already have, and make sure that you can recognize and remove any harmful relationships that might be dragging you down.

Having relationships doesn't just mean having friends to hang out with or family to live with. Relationships help us connect with other people and share our experiences, both good and bad. Crucially, relationships provide a foundation we can depend on. Whether you need someone to talk to, to listen, to make you laugh, or to provide a shoulder to cry on, relationships are fundamental. That's why having relationships is so important.

No matter how strong or independent someone might be, at some point they'll rely on others for support. Those others might support you materially, providing shelter, food, water, or clothing. They might support you emotionally, providing a space to express your emotions, be heard, and feel understood. They might support you mentally, helping you to destress, take a break, or blow off steam. In turn, you may be called on to support others, now or in the future. But everyone leans on others at some point. We are all interconnected.

MEASURE YOUR RELATIONSHIP NEEDS

While everyone has a need to belong, the ways in which people meet that need can be very different. Some people are extroverts. Extroverts are social butterflies; they like to be around people much or all of the time. They want to hang out or get together with friends often, and they may dislike spending time alone. Extroverts prefer to have lots of friends and to see them often. Other people are introverts. Introverts prefer to have fewer friends and a smaller social circle. They tend to value time alone or with only one or two others, and they often prefer to meet with friends in small groups. Just like extroverts, introverts have a need for social relationships; they simply go about forming relationships and meeting their needs in a different way. Of course, many people fall somewhere on a spectrum between these two extremes.

Understanding where you fall on this scale, whether you are more introverted or extroverted, can help you understand why you feel most comfortable in certain types of relationships. Are you more extroverted or introverted? Think about where you fall on the scale. If you prefer to have a large social circle, with lots of friends and plenty of chances to spend time with others, you are probably more extroverted, so you would place yourself closer to the extroverted end of the scale. If so, you can use the activities presented later in this chapter to help you expand your network, create connections with multiple people, and increase your social activity. If you prefer to have just a few close friends that you feel comfortable spending time with, you probably belong closer to the introverted end of the scale. If you are more introverted, you can use these same activities to deepen the relationships you have and focus on spending more time in smaller, more intimate settings.

RELATIONSHIPS ARE ALL AROUND US

If you stop to think about it, you'll realize you have many relationships in your life. There are family members: parents, grandparents, siblings, aunts and uncles, cousins, nieces and nephews. You might have friends, classmates, and teammates, maybe a romantic partner. You also have relationships with other people you meet: teachers, counselors, coaches, neighbors, bus drivers, religious or spiritual leaders, even the siblings and parents of your friends.

Relationships fill lots of different roles in your life. Some can be sources of support, encouragement, and friendship. Some relationships give you a person to talk to; others give you someone to go to for advice; still others provide a space where you can be your true self, without being judged. The list that follows suggests several different roles that people can play in your life.

- Someone who is a good listener/who tries to understand me

- Someone who gives me good advice

- Someone I have fun with, who makes me laugh

- Someone who encourages me

- Someone who loves me for who I am

- Someone I can share experiences with—the good and the bad

Take a minute to explore who fills each of these roles for you. It might be one person or more than one. There may be some roles for which you don't have any supportive relationships right now—that's okay, too. The next section will help you fill those gaps.

Over the next week, as you go about your life, take a few moments to think about the people you interact with throughout the day. You have relationships with all of these people, though some are certainly closer than others. For each of the people you interact with, consider whether they already fill one or more of the roles listed here for you. You may have more supportive relationships than you thought!

BUILDING YOUR SUPPORT SYSTEM

Getting the support you need when things get difficult requires two things. First, you need to have a supportive network. If you don't have people available to support you, then when things get difficult, you won't have someone to turn to for assistance. So ensuring that you have supportive people who can assist you is the first step.

The second step is to turn on—or *activate*—your support network. Having a network of supportive relationships is helpful only if you know how to get the support you need when you need it. Imagine for a moment that your home is on fire. You've gotten out, your family and pets are all safe, but the fire is getting bigger and bigger. What do you do next? You call the fire department to come put out the fire, right? If you don't call them, they won't know there's a fire to put out. Granted, the fire department might figure it out eventually even without your calling. They might see smoke in the distance and send a truck to see what's going on. Maybe a neighbor will notice the fire and call the fire department for you. But even though someone might notice and help, the best way to get the fire out is for *you* to call the fire department and alert them!

In the same way, if you don't alert your support people to let them know you need their support, then they won't know to come help you. Sometimes you might hint that you need support—you try to be subtle and give little clues. You might worry that you're asking too much of others. Or you might think that other people will be annoyed or angry with you for asking for help. In reality, many people are willing to help you; they just may not know that you need help—or what you need them to do. When a person isn't sure how to help someone, they may not help at all. Or they might try to help, but in a way that doesn't provide what you need. Activating your social support network requires being open and honest about what you need and how others can help. Once others know what you need and want, they can provide helpful support.

Learning to Ask for Support

How do you turn to your support network? The easiest and most effective way is to *ask* for the support and help you need. Asking for help can be scary, especially the first time you try it. To make it less scary and intimidating, it helps to know who you want to ask for support, what support you need, and how you'd like to say it. It is also helpful to ask for support *before* you desperately need it; that way your support team is in place when you need them and you can activate it more quickly. This section will take you through the steps for identifying a good support person and asking for support. At each step you'll make a detailed plan, writing out what you want to say so that you can practice ahead of time. Grab your journal and follow along, so you can start building your support team now.

Step 1. Choose a Type of Support to Seek

In the previous section, you explored the different supportive relationships you have in your life. Did you find any areas where you would like to have more support? Maybe you have lots of people to give you advice, but no one to just hang out with. Or maybe you have friends who are fun and make you laugh, but nobody to just listen and understand you. Use this activity to fill in any gaps in your support network. Is there a type of support that would be most helpful for you? Select the type you most want or need and use that as your focus for this activity. If you want more than one type of support, you can always repeat this activity later with a different type of support or a different target person.

Step 2: Identify a Support Person

Once you know what type of support you want or need, the next step is to identify a person who can provide it. This might be someone you know but haven't relied on for support before, or it could be someone already in your life. The key is to find someone who is a good fit for your needs. A good support person should be trustworthy. You should be comfortable talking to and spending time with them. Beyond that, try to find someone whose personality matches the role you want them to fill. For example, your fun-loving goofy friend might be a good person to fill the role of "someone I have fun with, who makes me laugh" but not the best person to fill the role of "someone who gives me advice." For that you might want someone older and wiser. Your favorite aunt, who is always available to provide encouragement, might also be a good person to fill the role of "someone who is a good listener, who tries to understand me." Think about who might be able to fill this role for you, and write down that person's name.

If you get stuck, there are a few strategies that can help you find a good support person. First, you might consider asking a parent, friend, school counselor, or spiritual leader to help you generate more ideas. Or you could try adopting a different perspective, as you did in chapter 3. Ask yourself, *If a friend was looking for someone to give them advice (or someone to just listen, encourage them, and so on), who would I suggest they talk to?* Then take your own suggestion. Finally, try observing others. Who do your friends or family members go to for support? Maybe their support people can act as your support people, too.

Step 3: Start a Conversation

Once you know *who* can give you the support you need, you can plan how to ask for that support. This can be one of the hardest parts—it can be really difficult to ask for help. One way is to start by letting the person know that you need to talk. For example, you could say, "Hey Aunt Rosa, do you have time to talk?" or, "Hey Mom, can we talk about something?" Take a moment to put this in your own words, and start writing out how you would say this.

Step 4: Express Your Feelings

Next, you want to let the person know how you are feeling. Try to do this using an *I-message*—a statement of your thoughts and feelings that focuses on your experience. For example, you could say "I've been feeling sad and lonely lately." or "Ever since the divorce, I'm feeling angry all the time." How would you express your feelings? Take a moment and put this into your own words. Be sure to use an emotion word! If you need some suggestions, refer back to the list of feelings words in chapter 3.

Step 5: State Your Needs Clearly

Now it's time to let this person know what you need. Be sure to use an I-message again. This is about your needs, so focus on what *you* want out of the relationship. For example, "I feel like what I really need right now is someone to talk to, someone who will just listen without giving me advice." Or "I think what I need right now is a friend who will help me get my mind off of my problems and make sure that I still have fun." Be sure to explain clearly how this person can help, by asking for what you need from them. You could say, "Could we take some time to do something fun?" or "Could you help me by just listening?" Again, put it in your own words, but remember to be direct and specific. Your goal is to be clear about the kind of support you need.

Step 6: Express Your Appreciation

Be sure to express your appreciation. A simple "Thank you" can have a big impact. People like to feel needed and appreciated. Saying "Thank you" lets people know that you value their help!

The figure is an example of how you might plan the six steps of asking for support. You can use this as a template for writing your plans in your journal.

Getting the Support I Need	
Step 1: Type of support I need:	
Someone who is a good listener/who tries to understand me. Someone who gives me good advice. Someone I have fun with, who makes me laugh.	Someone who encourages me. Someone who loves me for who I am. Someone I can share experiences with—the good and the bad.
Step 2: Who can provide support: Aunt Rosa	
Step 3: Start of the conversation: Hey Aunt Rosa, do you have a minute to talk?	
Step 4: Express my feelings: I've been having some trouble with my boyfriend lately.	
Step 5: Clearly state what I need: I'm hoping you can give me some relationship advice. Would you try and help me out?	
Step 6: Say thank you: I really appreciate your taking the time to give me advice. That was really helpful.	

Now that you have planned who to ask for support and how to ask them, it is important to follow through and have that talk. Sometimes it is helpful to *plan* exactly when you can do something. That way, you can be sure it will get done. *When do you plan on doing this?* What day? What time of day? Where will you be? Will you do this in person or over the phone? Give yourself a reminder. For keeping track of homework, you might use your school planner. Or you might keep track of important dates on a calendar. Writing things down or putting a reminder on your phone can help make sure you don't forget about it. Take a few minutes to plan when you will ask for support. Then make sure to follow through and give it a try!

What to Do When Your Support Doesn't Show Up

Sometimes someone you rely on for support may not show up and support you in the way that you need. Maybe they were busy with other things, had concerns of their own, or were struggling with their own stresses. Maybe you thought you clearly expressed your need but they didn't understand what you needed. Maybe they were simply out of town. Our support people are human, too! They make mistakes, get overwhelmed, and sometimes let us down unintentionally. When that happens, it is important to do two things:

- Cut them some slack. Just because they didn't help you this time doesn't mean they won't help in the future. Their failure may have nothing to do with you. Maybe they would love to support you but just can't do it right now. Keep them on your support team, but continue your quest to get the support you need.

- Select another support person and try again. Repeat as often as needed until you find a support person who can fulfill your needs. When it comes to supportive relationships, it's important to have a deep bench. Keep trying until your needs are met.

STRENGTHEN YOUR EXISTING RELATIONSHIPS

Relationships need to be nurtured. It takes time and energy to build good, strong relationships. Much as plants need water and sunlight to grow and bloom, relationships need our attention and care to become strong and reliable. Imagine if you bought a plant and put it in your room. At first, it might make the space feel welcoming and alive. But if you never water it, never give it sunlight or fertilizer, and never give it the attention it needs, it isn't going to survive for long. Relationships are the same way—but instead of water and sunlight, they need time and attention. To ensure you have strong relationships, it's important to spend time building and strengthening your bonds with other people. That way, when times are tough and you need support, you have people you can rely on.

Consider the story of Daniel.

Daniel, age fifteen, has just moved to a new town and started at a new high school. He's now far away from his old friends, including his best friend, Raquel. Raquel used to always give Daniel great advice, especially when it came to dealing with his parents. While Daniel and Raquel still talk, it's been harder to stay in touch. They certainly don't talk as much as they used to. Lately, Daniel has been turning to his cousin Maikel for advice. He really values his friendship with Maikel and appreciates his help. So Daniel decides to strengthen his relationship with Maikel. He plans a movie night just for the two of them. He bakes cookies and makes popcorn. They spend the evening watching movies and talking about the soccer, school, and plans for the summer. By planning a movie night, Daniel and Maikel strengthened their relationship. Maybe one movie night made only a little bit of a difference, but it's a good start. Over the next several weeks, they continue to hang out and spend time together, and their relationship continues to strengthen. As they become closer, Daniel knows he has a true friend he can rely on—and who relies on him, too.

Building relationships takes time. It certainly doesn't happen overnight! But with time and effort, building relationships can be extremely rewarding.

Relationships help you connect to others and find a place where you can belong and feel free to be yourself.

Make a Plan to Strengthen Your Relationships

It's never too soon to start actively working to build and strengthen your relationships. A little bit of planning and effort can make a huge difference. So grab your journal and follow along.

Step 1: Pick a Relationship to Strengthen

Think about which relationship you would like to focus on. Maybe you have a friend you really like but haven't seen in a while. Or maybe you enjoy spending time with your siblings, cousins, or neighbors. Which of your relationships would you most like to spend some time strengthening?

Now examine your relationship with this person. What makes this relationship worth working on? What is it about this person that you like? Write down why this relationship is important to you and why you value your relationship with this person.

Step 2: Generate Ideas

Now that you've explored your relationship a bit, use that information to make some plans. One of the best ways to strengthen a relationship is to spend time with someone in an activity you'll both enjoy. What sort of things could you do to spend time with this person? Use what you know about them and the things you've done together in the past to help generate ideas. What sort of things have you done together? What are some of the good times you have had with this person? And remember, spending time with someone doesn't have to cost money—many of the best things you can do are free!

Here are some more ideas—if any of these seem good to you, add them to your list.

Strengthen Your Relationships by Spending Time Together		
Doing Fun Things Together	Making Time to Talk	Going Places
Toss around a football	Go for a walk	Visit the zoo
Plan a party	Take your dogs to the park	Go to a sports event
Start an art project	Have a picnic	Go out to the movies
Play games	Go for a jog	Hang out by the pool
Rearrange a room	Grab coffee or tea	Plan a day trip
Have a movie night	Go out for ice cream	Volunteer together

Step 3: Select an Activity

Now that you have a list, take a look at each of the ideas you came up with. Think about how easy or difficult it would be to do each of them. For example, going out to the movies might require finding a ride to the theater and paying for tickets and snacks—resources you may or may not have at this moment. On the other hand, having a movie night at home or going to the park to play basketball might be easier to plan. Put a star by each of things that you think would be easy for you to plan and arrange.

Finally, it's time to pick something! Select one of the activities you put a star on and ask this person if they'd like to do that thing. If, like Daniel, you picked a movie night, invite that person over to watch a movie. If you picked an activity like playing basketball, text your person to ask them if they'd like to play basketball some time. Be open to alternative suggestions and try to be flexible with your schedule. The important thing is to spend quality time with someone; your list of ideas is just a starting point.

Step 4: Make It Happen

Be sure to follow through! As with so many things in this book, the real impact happens when you follow through and do the activities you've planned. Take a moment to plan when this is going to happen. Call or text this person, find a time, and make room in your schedule. If you need permission from a parent or guardian, be sure to ask them first. If you need supplies (like popcorn for movie night), set yourself a reminder to gather these.

Keep in mind, this isn't a one-time thing. To keep your relationships strong, you'll need to regularly set aside time to spend with other people. Staying actively engaged in your relationships—spending time with others and being together—should be a part of your usual routine. It might help to block off time in your calendar, make plans in advance, or keep at least one evening a week clear for spending time with other people. You may have lots of other demands on your time, like school, homework, a part-time job, or work around the house. Still, by staying active in your relationships, you'll build and strengthen your sense of connection and belonging.

YOU ARE NOT A BURDEN

Teens who have thoughts of suicide can often feel like they are a burden on others (Joiner, 2005). A burden is like a heavy weight, something that pulls us down or makes things worse in our lives. *Burdensomeness* is the sense that you are making things more difficult for others or that others would be better off without you. In our work with teens who have felt like a burden on others, common themes include thinking they are disappointing family members by disobeying or getting into trouble, posing a financial burden to the family, or taking up too much of others' time. These themes share a sense of taking more from others than you contribute to them—costing more to others than you give back in return.

Burdensomeness is sneaky. It creeps up on you and makes you forget all of the ways that you contribute to other people's lives. It can make you feel like your worth—and the value of your life—is based on what you give to other people. But it also makes you forget all the things you do that make people value and appreciate you: being a friend, telling a joke, listening to others, helping someone relax or have some fun. Just being there—and being you—is often so valued by others that they *don't* feel like you are a burden. Recognizing your value to others, to the people in your life, can help to balance out thoughts of being a burden.

Relationships are a two-way street. We call on our friends and family to support us in times of need; in turn, we also support them when they need help. Maybe you helped them in the past, or maybe you will help them sometime in the future. Maybe they help you in one way and you help them in another. When people feel like a burden on others, they are seeing their relationships as being one-way—like they are receiving support but not giving it back. This can blind you to the other half of the equation. So when you feel like a burden on others, remember that the relationships you have been building and strengthening work both ways. Maybe you need more support right now, but someday you'll be the one supporting others in need. You'll pay it forward in the future.

Journal in hand, take a few minutes to think back on all the ways you've helped others in the past. Have you helped around the house? Listened when a friend needed to vent? Taken care of a neighbor's dog? Mowed the lawn or shoveled snow? Also think about the ways you might contribute in the future. Make a list to remind yourself of the ways you have contributed to others or plan to.

PRUNING UNHEALTHY RELATIONSHIPS

Just as it is important to strengthen relationships to improve our sense of connection and belongingness, it can also be important to know when a relationship is unhealthy and needs to be removed. Think of your relationships like a garden. The flowers and plants that you want in your garden need to be taken care of and nurtured so they grow up strong and healthy. But sometimes there are weeds in your garden. If they grow too big, they start taking the water, light, and nutrients that the other plants need. They can crowd out the other plants and ruin your garden. As the gardener, you need to remove a weed before it gets too big and starts to cause problems.

In the same way, negative or unhealthy relationships—the weeds in your garden—can hurt you and leave you feeling isolated, unloved, or unlovable. It is important to put a stop to harmful relationships. That means removing yourself from situations or relationships that are unhealthy or abusive.

Spotting the Weeds

Identifying which of your relationships are unhealthy can be challenging. Some unhealthy relationships are easy to spot—like a bully at school or an online troll. Others can be more difficult to identify. Often, that's because the relationship didn't start out unhealthy but became that way over time. To continue the metaphor of a garden, the first few green shoots that poke up through the soil might be flowers or weeds. Often you can't tell which they are until they start growing. Unhealthy relationships can appear healthy at first, like a new relationship that feels good but later turns jealous and controlling. Unhealthy relationships can also be difficult to spot when they are mixed— making you feel good sometimes and awful at other times.

At their core, unhealthy relationships are those with people who don't respect or value your worth as a human being. In an unhealthy relationship, the other shows disrespect for your ability to make decisions for yourself. They can also be controlling; they may try to dictate what you are or are not allowed to do. Of course, as you are a teenager, there must be some healthy controls or limits. You can't buy alcohol; you might have a curfew, or you might not be allowed to go certain places (for example, you may not be able to get into R-rated movies). These sorts of limitations are typical for teens; they are designed to protect you and keep you safe. But other types of control are not healthy.

So how do you know when signs of disrespect or control are part of an unhealthy relationship, whether it's a romantic relationship, friendship, or otherwise? Here are some signs that a relationship is unhealthy—and might be in need of weed removal (Interagency Working Group on Youth Programs, 2021; National Domestic Violence Hotline, 2021; Planned Parenthood Federation of America Inc., 2021):

- *Control.* When someone makes all the decisions and tells you what to do, what to wear, or who to spend time with. A dating partner might try to pass this off as jealousy, but this may really be an attempt to isolate you from your friends and family.

- *Dishonesty.* When someone lies to you or keeps information from you.

- *Disrespect.* When someone makes fun of your opinions and interests or destroys something that belongs to you.

- *Intimidation.* When someone tries to control aspects of your life by making you afraid of them or what they threaten to do. They might threaten to hurt themself or someone else if you leave them or go against their wishes. Threats of violence are *never* acceptable.

- *Physical or sexual violence.* When someone uses force to get their way or pressures you into sexual activity without your free and willing consent.

Maybe you've looked at that list and are still not sure which of your relationships might be unhealthy. That's okay—it can be difficult to spot unhealthy relationships from the inside. It's not easy to determine whether a relationship is unhealthy or is just going through a difficult patch. Here are some other relationship red flags that can help you decide. If the person does any of the following, these are red flags indicating the relationship is unhealthy.

- Shows extreme jealousy of your friends or tells you who you can spend time with.

- Has a bad temper, so you are afraid to make them angry.

- Checks your text or social media messages without your permission.

- Pressures you to have sex, use drugs or alcohol, or do other things you aren't comfortable with.

- Insults, demeans, or shames you, especially in front of other people.

- Threatens you with violence.

- Prevents you from making your own decisions.

- Destroys your belongings.

- Threatens to "out" you or tell your secrets.

- Puts you down or says that you never do anything right.

After looking over this list, do you have any relationships that you think might be unhealthy? If you still aren't sure, ask a trusted adult for support and advice. It is often easier for someone outside an unhealthy relationship to see the problem. Talking to a trusted adult could help you get a different perspective. You can also look back at chapter 3, where you learned about adopting a different perspective. Consider what advice you would give to a friend who was in your situation. Would you think the relationship looks unhealthy from the outside? If so, it probably is.

It is important to always remember that you are not to blame if a relationship is unhealthy. It is *not* your fault. It may be tough to see that from the inside, but unhealthy relationships aren't your doing. But you can do something about them: You can get out.

Pulling the Weeds

Once you've spotted an unhealthy relationship, it's time to pull the weeds. But getting yourself out of an unhealthy relationship can be difficult. Let's return to Daniel, whom we met earlier, to see how he handles an unhealthy relationship.

Daniel is having some difficulty with his boyfriend, James. Daniel and James have been going out for about four months now. Lately, it seems to Daniel like he can't do anything right in their relationship. It feels like everything he does upsets James and starts an argument. These arguments always leave Daniel feeling worthless and depressed. Working extra hours at his job, hanging out with his cousin, even spending time with his friends from school—doing any of these things seem to make James mad. James always decides where they go and what they do. And lately Daniel has felt pressured to do some things he isn't comfortable with.

After reviewing the list of relationship red flags, Daniel realizes that his relationship with his boyfriend isn't very healthy. Daniel sees now that it isn't something *he* did and it isn't something wrong with him. Being in an unhealthy relationship isn't his fault. But he needs to get out of the relationship and doesn't know what to do! Daniel is afraid that if he tries to break up with James, it'll go badly. He doesn't know what James will do—and he doesn't know if he can stick to his decision. He decides to ask his dad for advice. Daniel's dad suggests he break up via text message. "I know," his dad admits, "a text message feels like a bad way to break up, but in this case, I think that's the safest way to do it. Breaking up is difficult, but don't let him talk you out of it. Stick close to your friends at school and avoid him. Your safety and your health are the most important thing."

Daniel did a lot of things right: He recognized an unhealthy relationship—in this case, a romantic relationship with his boyfriend James. He realized he needed to get out and that being in an unhealthy relationship isn't his fault. Then, when he got stuck, he got help from someone he trusted. Now that Daniel has a plan, he needs to stick to it and end this unhealthy relationship for good.

So how do you get out of a difficult and unhealthy relationship? There are a few different ways that might work, but you'll have to pick the one that seems best to you. Let's review a couple of different methods for getting out of unhealthy relationships.

- *The Confrontation:* This is the most direct way to end a relationship. You can end a friendship or break up with someone you are dating by simply telling that person the relationship is over. This method should be used only when it is safe to do so—when this person is not likely to react violently—and when you are confident in your ability to follow through (and not be talked out of it).

- *The Assist:* This one is particularly useful for unhealthy friendships. You can ask a trusted adult to assist you in ending the relationship. You could ask your parent to "forbid you to see" a person or "not allow them to come over any more"—which can be an excuse to end the relationship. You can also ask teachers to move your seat in class, or employers to schedule you on different shifts, to try to increase the distance between you and an unhealthy relationship partner. Ending relationships can feel difficult and overwhelming, so getting an assist from a trusted adult can help make things easier.

An assist can also be used to force a relationship to change. If the relationship is with a coworker, a rude boss, or a mean teacher, getting someone to help you express your concerns can be helpful. In a workplace, it might involve a human resources person. Schools don't usually have someone like that, but a teacher, counselor, or principal could likely give you an assist.

- *The Fadeout:* A less direct way of ending a relationship, in the fadeout you spend less and less time with this person, until you rarely or never see them or speak to them. This works for all kinds of relationships. Make excuses to avoid them; keep yourself busy with other, healthier relationships; and slowly end all contact with them. This method should be used only when you are *not* in danger of being abused by this person.

- *The Ghost:* A more abrupt version of the fadeout, you can end a friendship or romantic relationship more quickly by ghosting the person—breaking off all contact, not answering messages or texts, and avoiding them. Ghosting is most useful for ending unhealthy or dangerous relationships quickly and without confrontation. If you'll see this person often, like at school or work, ghosting probably isn't your best option.

Because relationships are so important, unhealthy relationships can be extremely hurtful. Recognizing unhealthy relationships and rooting them out is an important skill to have. Whether it's a friend, dating partner, school bully, or disrespectful teacher or boss, recognizing when someone isn't treating you with respect and value is key. As a teenager, you may not have complete control over who you encounter in your life, but you can take steps to get out of bad relationships and replace them with friends you choose—people who are supportive and who make you feel valued. Getting out of unhealthy, toxic relationships can also make you feel happier, less stressed, and less anxious.

COPING WITH LOSS

You've just seen the importance of ending unhealthy relationships. Sometimes ending a relationship isn't our choice. Sometimes healthy relationships end before we are ready. One of the most challenging experiences you can face is losing someone you are close to. It could be a friendship or romantic relationship that came to an end, moving to a new city and losing contact with your friends, or even the death of someone you care about. There's no easy solution for learning to cope with loss, but there are some things that can help.

Remember: The Pain Isn't Permanent

Loss comes in many forms—breakups, growing apart, moving away, divorce, and death—and each brings unique emotions that can seem overwhelmingly powerful. And each person responds differently to losing someone they love. While everyone's situation is different and everyone reacts differently to losing a loved one, there are some common thoughts and feelings that many people share. You might feel sadness, depression, or even despair. You might find yourself becoming angry and upset, feeling like you've been cheated out of a relationship that should have lasted much longer. You might feel overwhelmed, shocked, or stunned. You might feel relieved, guilty, or like you're all alone in the world. Most likely, you'll feel several of these things all at once. All of the emotions, thoughts, and experiences you have after losing someone you felt close to can be called *grief*.

Sometimes it feels like your grief will go on forever. But recall how in chapter 3 you learned about recognizing and responding to different emotions.

You practiced several different skills for managing strong feelings. This is proof that emotions can change. With time, strong emotions will become less overwhelming. As time passes, you'll find yourself going about your day and returning to your new normal. That doesn't mean you have to forget the person you lost, or that you love them any less. This is a normal part of the grieving process.

If you've lost someone you really care about, think about the way it felt at first. What emotions did you feel, and how strong were they? Take a minute or two and make a list of what you felt and how powerful those emotions were. Do you still feel all of those things? Are the emotions as strong now as they were when you first lost this person? Or have they changed over time? If you find that your emotions are just as strong now as they were when you first lost this person—especially if it has been months or even years since it happened—you may benefit from additional care and support for managing your grief. Look for a local support group or professional; you'll also find support groups online. (For more information on seeking a professional, check out chapter 8.)

Create a Memorial

For many young people, death is a particularly difficult type of loss to cope with. When someone you are close to dies, it can be helpful to find a way to remember them. You might fear that, over time, you'll forget about the person, that you won't remember what they looked like or sounded like, or the good times you had together. One way to ensure that you remember this person is to create a memorial. A memorial can come in many forms. You could fill a box with mementos that help preserve good memories of the person. It could be a collection of photographs stored in your phone or on your computer. It could be a scrapbook or journal where you record your good memories.

Creating a memorial doesn't have to be complicated. A simple memorial is one of the best ways to remember a person. Use the following steps to create a memorial for someone you've lost and want to remember (Hill et al., 2019):

1. Start by finding the right box: a shoebox or shipping box of the right size.

2. Give it a cover—draw a picture or design an image to put on the top. This cover can be simple or as creative and fanciful as you like! If you like to sketch or draw, you could do this by hand. If you like to work on a computer, create an image with photo editing software.

3. Add a couple of photographs that capture the person's personality and shared experiences. If you don't have any photographs, ask a family member or friend who might have some.

4. Find some scraps of colorful paper, small notecards, or sticky notes and write down some of the things you loved most about this person. Think about their good qualities—their kindness, honesty, humor, or other positive features you'll miss—and write them down on different pieces of paper. Place these in the box.

5. Next, record some of your favorite memories of this person. Write or draw each on a different piece of paper or notecard. Include only good memories—the ones that put a smile on your face.

6. Add any additional items that help you to remember this person in a positive way. These might be small keepsakes or tokens that evoke memories or say something positive about them.

That's your memorial! Whenever you miss this person, you can visit this box. Reading through some of your favorite memories can help you to hold on to the good times you had with this person and remember why you loved them. With the help of your memorial, your relationship with this person lives on, through your memories and emotions.

MOVING FORWARD

In this chapter, you learned a lot about relationships and how incredibly important they are. You explored the human need to belong and to have satisfying relationships. Just as food, water, and shelter are vital to keep us physically healthy, we need relationships to keep ourselves mentally healthy. To help with building your relationships, you explored how to ask for support and assistance when you need it. You also explored how to create connections with others and strengthen your relationships. You learned how to spot toxic, unhealthy relationships and how to extricate yourself from them safely. Finally, you learned a bit about how to manage one of the most painful relationship difficulties of all—losing a loved one. All of these skills and activities are part of building and maintaining social supports and healthy relationships, so you feel connected to others.

CHAPTER 7

Building Purpose

Thoughts of suicide are often most intense when you feel overwhelmed, trapped, or out of options. At times like that, it can seem like suicide is the only way out of an unbearable situation. Yet when you picked up this book you made a decision—whether you realized it or not—to fight against your thoughts of suicide. Every time you read more of this book, try one of the suggested activities, or practice a new skill, you are making that same decision—to stand up and fight back. Regardless of how you came to this book, by committing to making an effort, you've made a statement that you want to overcome thoughts of suicide and keep on living.

This chapter asks the question: *What made you take that step?* What makes you want to continue fighting, even when life seems overwhelming and suicide seems like the only option? Logically, there *must* be an answer, though it may be difficult for you to put into words. Someone who had no hope, who had totally given up, wouldn't continue to try and make things better. But here you are, working to create a life you want to live. Clearly there is something in your life that makes it worth living. Maybe you know exactly what is driving you toward life. Or maybe you haven't figured out what it is yet. Whatever the case, in this chapter you'll focus on *what makes life worth living*. If you don't know yet why you started this book or what makes your life worth living, in this chapter we'll help you find out.

In previous chapters, the focus was on managing your thoughts of suicide and the emotions, thoughts, and stresses that drive them. You were working to reduce the things that drive you toward death. In this section, you'll approach the issue from a different perspective—by working to build up the things that drive you toward life and living. These *reasons for living* can be nearly anything: relationships that you value, things you want to accomplish, places you want to go, an impact you want to have on the world, or a belief in the inherent value of life. In this chapter, you'll start by exploring your reasons for living. Then you'll learn how to use your reasons for living to set goals and live in a way that aligns with your beliefs and desires. In short, you'll work toward a life that has purpose and direction.

DISCOVER YOUR REASONS FOR LIVING

In this section, you'll start to explore your reasons for living and hopefully discover some new ones along the way. Reasons for living must be personal. Each of us has different reasons for living. You might come up with lots of them, or you might struggle to find even one or two. Don't force it. The most important thing about listing your reasons for living is that they have to be *yours*. They have to be reasons that you come up with. They should be things that you value or people you care about. If your list of reasons for living isn't specific to what you value and care about, then those reasons aren't going to ring true. They'll feel false—and they won't help support you when you need a reason to keep on fighting.

Take a look at Jaysen's and Alicia's situations and try to imagine what their reasons for living might be:

> Jaysen is a freshman in high school and the youngest of three siblings. Jaysen's entire family is obsessed with baseball. His father is the varsity baseball coach; his mother is an umpire. His older sister played varsity softball and now plays for the local university. Jaysen is on the junior varsity team at his high school. He's played baseball his entire life. He

played T-ball and slow-pitch softball in elementary school. He played in junior high school. He went to baseball summer camps. And as you might imagine, thanks to all that practice and experience, Jaysen is really good.

You might expect that Jaysen would list baseball as one of his reasons for living. Surely he must love the game, right? And maybe Jaysen *would* list baseball as one of his reasons for living. Maybe he loves playing so much that it does make life worth living. But what if he doesn't truly love the sport? Or, at least, what if he doesn't love it enough that it drives him to keep on living? Maybe Jaysen plays baseball only because he is expected to, because he loves his family and they connect over baseball, or because he enjoys spending time with his teammates. In that case, instead of listing baseball as a reason for living, he might list his family or his friendships with teammates as reasons for living.

Alicia is about to graduate from high school. She works two evenings a week as a server at the local diner. She doesn't have any idea what she wants to do after high school. She's thought about going to college, but none of the majors spark any real interest for her. Alicia figures that she'll probably just pick up more shifts at the diner, but that's not really what she wants either. Her future seems so unclear and hazy. Alicia doesn't see anything worth living for.

It might seem like Alicia doesn't have any reasons for living at all. With a little guidance from her counselor she comes to realize that what she likes about working as a server is helping others to have a fun night out. She realizes that she is also a bit of a foodie and enjoys cooking at home. Alicia decides that she'd like to combine those two things and try to become a cook at the diner this summer. She's even considering going to culinary school to become a professional cook or caterer. For Alicia, having a direction in life is particularly important. Now that she has found a career path of interest to her and some goals to work toward, she feels like she has some reasons for living.

Perhaps, like Jaysen, you have reasons for living that might not be obvious to others. Or, like Alicia, your reasons for living might not be obvious to you and might require some exploration. In Jaysen's case, his family and friends might have guessed that baseball was his driving force, when it was actually relationships that he valued most. For Alicia, finding reasons for living required looking more closely to discover what she is passionate about. Finding your reasons for living will require looking inward, thinking carefully about what drives you. Maybe your reasons are clear to you. Or maybe you'll need to work to discover them. Chances are you've never been asked, straight out, "What are your reasons for living?" So if you get stuck or have trouble thinking of reasons, that's okay! We will continue to explore possible reasons for living in the next section.

A good place to start is to explore the reasons for living that you may have already. Then you'll explore common reasons for living that many people express, to see if you can discover others. So before we go any further, grab your journal and spend a little time thinking about and answering these questions:

- What is it that keeps you alive?

- What is the most important thing in your life right now?

- What is one thing, person, or activity that you could never give up?

- What things are important enough to you that you're willing to keep on living, even when you are hurting and in pain?

- Who—or what—do you care about enough to keep up the fight against suicidal thoughts?

Take some time and make a list, identifying as many reasons as you can.

Now let's explore some of the most common reasons for living that teens often mention. If any of these resonate with you, add them to your list.

Important Relationships

Some of the most powerful reasons for living are the people you care about. Maybe you want to make your mom or dad proud of you. Maybe you want to set a good example for your younger sibling or cousin. Maybe there's a classmate or neighbor you look out for or protect. Maybe there is a parent, grandparent, sibling, cousin, aunt, uncle, niece, or nephew who would miss you if you were gone. This could be someone who looks up to you, relies on you, loves you, and enjoys talking to you. Or it could be someone you look up to, someone you want to be like, or someone you want to spend more time with. Maybe you have a dog or cat who would feel abandoned if you were gone—and who wouldn't understand why you weren't there. Family, friends, neighbors, classmates, teammates, coworkers, and pets—any or all of these relationships can serve as an anchor, helping us to hold onto life. Take a few minutes to explore what relationships are your reasons for living, and add them to your list.

Future Goals

Your goals for the future can also be reasons for living. This could be things you want to do in life, career goals, things you would like to accomplish, or places you want to visit. Do you want to graduate high school, go to college, or find a job that you love? Do you want to get your own place? Have a family? Do you want to move across the country? Do you want to visit Paris, London, or Rio de Janeiro? Do you want to see the Pyramids, go on a safari, or walk on the Great Wall of China? Do you want to go swimming in Australia, surfing in California, or hiking on the Appalachian Trail? Do you want to win an award, become a DJ, coach a sports team, become a chef, or build a car from scratch? Think about the things you want to do with your life. Goals and dreams give us something to aim for and work toward. Take a few minutes to explore the goals and dreams that make life worth living for you. Add them to your list.

Spiritual Beliefs

What do your spiritual beliefs say about suicide? Spiritual beliefs might be based on your religion or on personal beliefs about what is right or wrong, the value of your life, and the importance of facing down difficult times. What do your beliefs say about suicide, self-harm, or having hope for the future? Take a few minutes to explore your spiritual beliefs, and if any are reasons for living, add them to your list.

Things You are Passionate About

Sometimes the things you enjoy can be reasons for living on their own. Your reasons for living might include things that you really love doing, that bring you joy and pleasure. This might be a favorite sport, making music, or creating art. It could be dance, drawing, decorating, photography, fashion design, woodworking, sculpting, or gardening. It might be that you take pleasure in mathematics, in reading or writing fantastic stories, being in nature, or building things. Maybe you are passionate about helping others, volunteering, or helping animals. Think about the things you enjoy doing. Are there things you enjoy enough that it would be worth living just to get to do them again? Take a few minutes to explore your passions, and if any are reasons for living, add them to your list.

Hope for the Future

Hope is a belief that no matter how bad things might be right now, they will get better. Hope is trusting that tough times will eventually pass. Hope is the belief that there will be happier times ahead. Hope is the knowledge that, no matter what you are going through, it is possible to make a better, brighter future. Maybe you aren't sure what your reason for living is, but you just know that you have one. When your reason for living is difficult to define or hard to put into words, it might be simplest just to say that you have hope that things will get better. A sense of hope can be a fantastic source of strength. If this resonates with you, then add "hope" to your list of reasons for living.

Once you have listed as many reasons for living as you can think of, take a look at the following list of potential reasons for living. Do you share any of these? If so, add them to your list.

Possible Reasons for Living

- How your family would miss you

- Graduating from high school

- A friend's reliance on you

- Going to college

- Being a good role model for a sibling/cousin

- Having a career you love

- How abandoned your pets would feel

- Wanting to make your parents proud

- Religious teaching against suicide

- Hobbies that make you happy

- A place you want to visit

- A goal you want to accomplish

- A change you want to create in the world

- Something you want to do in life

Finally, when you've completed your list as best you can, take a few minutes to review the reasons you've listed. Do you see any common themes? Are there any patterns? Maybe your reasons for living are centered on something you want to accomplish, like going to college, having a career, having a family of your own. Maybe your reasons for living are centered on relationships that are important to you. Remembering your reasons for living can help give you strength and purpose when you have thoughts of suicide. Keep this list around for later! Take a picture and store it in your phone. Tape the list to your bathroom mirror, next to your bed, or on your bedroom door. Remind yourself every day of the reasons why life is worth living.

Your reasons for living don't have to be picture-perfect relationships or elaborate goals for the future. In fact, you can be sure that you'll experience challenges related to your reasons for living from time to time. For example, if one of your reasons for living is a relationship, you may have an intense argument with your loved one, go through difficult times with them, or not always see eye to eye. If one of your reasons for living is a goal or something you want to accomplish, you can anticipate some difficulty or failure along the way, like not getting accepted into your first-choice college, or struggling to learn a new skill. You get the idea. Challenges are normal and to be expected—they're part of life. What's important is selecting reasons for living that you care about.

FINDING WHAT MATTERS TO YOU

Now that you've explored your reasons for living, the rest of this chapter will focus on helping you turn your reasons for living into a life with purpose and meaning. Living life with purpose is about trying to achieve goals and doing things that are important to you. If you are trying to achieve goals that *you* think are important, that are in line with your personal values, the act of working on those goals will be more fulfilling.

Here are three activities to help you think about what is important to you and brainstorm some goals. Later you will refine those goals and turn them into specific action steps that you can work toward. Of course, you don't need to plan out your entire life! Nobody can tell the future, after all. Instead, think about what you value and what you want out of life, at least for the next few months or years. This will give you direction. And remember, you can always revise your goals later on.

Activity 1: Work from Your Reasons for Living

The first way to identify goals that are important to you is to take a look at the reasons for living you identified in the last section. Are any of these based on future goals? Reasons for living like "go to college" or "become an engineer" are goals all by themselves.

Other reasons for living can help you to set goals. If any revolve around important relationships, think about goals you might have for those relationships. For example, if your reason for living is your grandmother, what might that mean for you? Maybe you want to spend more time with her, or have her teach you her favorite recipes. Or consider a reason for living like "be there for my younger brother." What might that look like? Maybe that means teaching him how to play your favorite video game or being around to help him with his homework. It might mean being a role model for him, by finishing high school, going to college, and working hard. Maybe it means being his friend, so he has someone to give him advice.

Think about what each of your reasons for living means to you, and list a goal for each. If your reasons include activities you enjoy or love to do, then consider setting goals like making time for that activity or developing a new skill. If playing basketball was your reason for living, your goals might include "getting better at free throws" or "spending more time with your teammates."

Activity 2: Explore Your Beliefs and Values

Another great way to identify the things that matter to you—and to create goals for life—is to consider your most important values. You've probably never been asked to think about your values before. Identifying personal values isn't the sort of thing covered in school. But exploring your values can help you identify what you feel is important. Take a look at this list of values and think about what each one means to you.

Personal Values		
Family	Honesty	Courage
Kindness	Loyalty	Wellness
Intelligence	Communication	Creativity
Success	Integrity	Wealth
Spirituality	Leadership	Cooperation
Diversity	Generosity	Self-Expression

Think of it this way: If someone asked your best friend to pick the three values that best describe you, what would you want your friend to say? Would you want them to describe you as generous, honest, and creative? Or would you like them to call you successful, hard-working, and loyal? Thinking about how you want others to describe you can help you pick out the values that are most important to you.

As you select the values that mean the most to you, think about the ways you can live these values in your day-to-day life. If you selected creativity as one of your values, what would that mean to your life? How can you find a little bit of time each day to express your creativity? Could you spend some time each day in art or writing? Could you learn a new skill or craft? Maybe you want to learn more about graphic design or animation. If success is one of your values, what does that mean to you? Maybe that means finishing high school, going to college, and making a lot of money. Maybe it means doing really well at a particular sport or activity. Maybe it means getting a part-time job and getting some work experience. Identifying the values that matter to you can help you to set goals for your life that have meaning and worth for you.

Activity 3: Create a Vision for Your Future

Consider Tsula's story:

Tsula is sixteen and a junior in high school. In a meeting with her school academic counselor, Tsula explored her interests and·goals for after high school and her career. She had never really thought much about what would happen after high school. With the help of her counselor, Tsula explored some of her likes and dislikes. She loves reading the local newspaper. She loves telling stories and listening to the stories of others. On the other hand, she despises everything related to math and numbers. She would be perfectly happy to never see another equation after high school! Tsula also explored her core beliefs—the things she is passionate about. She realized that she has a strong belief that *people should tell the truth, no matter what.* Based on her love of storytelling, the news, and finding out the truth of things, Tsula decides that she wants to be·a journalist. So she sets a goal to begin doing the things that make for a good journalist: reading the newspaper, writing stories, and preparing for college. Now Tsula tries to do something each day related to her goal of becoming a journalist. Even if it is only for a few minutes, it helps Tsula feel like she is making progress toward her goal of becoming a journalist and telling the truth to the world!

Just like Tsula, you need to take time and think about what matters the most to you. What do you want to accomplish in the future? What are your goals or desires? Think about the things that matter to you and make a list in your journal.

Try this: At some point, someone has probably asked you the question: *What do you want to be when you grow up?* Take a minute, close your eyes, and visualize or imagine what you want life to look like ten or twenty years from now. What sort of work are you doing? Where do you live? Do you have a family? Are you married? Dating? Do you have children? Do you have a dog, cat, or hamster? What do you do for fun? Do you hang out with friends or go for walks? Do you travel to visit amazing places? Have you accomplished things? Picture the kind of life you want for yourself. When you have an image in your mind, describe it! Try to put that image into words. The things you pictured in your mind can become goals for the future.

Creating Goals Based on What Is Important to You	
Starting Point	Goals
Work from Your Reasons for Living	
Become a graphic designer.	1. Learn how to design websites online. 2. Spend time digitally editing photos.
Make Grandpa proud of me.	1. Study and do well in school. 2. Spend time with Grandpa on Saturdays.
Explore Your Beliefs and Values	
I value family.	1. Set up a game night with my family. 2. Ask Grandma to teach me how to bake.
I value creativity.	1. Write in my journal every day. 2. Start a journal of my sketches.
Create a Vision for Your Future	
Graduate high school and go to college.	1. Spend time studying each evening. 2. Look up colleges and application due dates.

HOW TO SET GOALS: BE SMART ABOUT IT

Now that you've thought about what is important to you and set some goals for yourself, it's *almost* time to starting working toward them. But first, it's helpful to spend some time revisiting your goals. Often, when people set goals, they pick ones that are unclear, too big, or too far off in the future. Revising your goals so that you have a clear path forward can help set you up for success.

The *way* you set goals affects your chances of success or failure. When goals are vague or hard to measure, like "Do better at school" or "Improve my relationship with Mom," it's hard to tell when you've accomplished your goal. When goals are too big or too far in the future, like "Become a doctor and help people," you won't know what steps to take to get there—and you might give up. Setting good goals ensures that you know what your goal is, how to achieve it, and how to know when you're done and can celebrate. The key to setting good goals: Make them SMART goals.

The SMART acronym stands for Specific, Measurable, Attainable, Relevant, and Time-Bound. Creating goals with these five points in mind helps to make sure you can achieve your goals. Let's review each of these five points in turn. Select one of the goals you identified in the previous section and use it as an example, turning it into a SMART goal as you go.

S Is for Specific

When a goal is vague or fuzzy, it can be difficult to know what steps you need to take to achieve it. When a goal is too broad or big, it might require so many steps to reach it that you feel overwhelmed. So the first step in creating SMART goals is to make sure your goal is specific. For example, the goal "Do better in school" isn't very specific. Are you focused on your grades, your attendance, or not getting into trouble with teachers? Do you want better grades in all your classes or just in one or two specific classes? What would it mean to do better in your classes? Do you need to get an A, or would a B or C be fine?

Instead of "Do better in school," you might try "Get a B in chemistry." Sometimes making goals more specific also means breaking big goals down into smaller goals. So you might change "Do better in school" into "Get a B in chemistry" *and* "Get a C in history." Now you have two goals, but each is specific. With these specific goals, you have a clearer sense of what you are aiming for. You'll also be better able to tell when you have completed each goal. A good way to evaluate whether your goal is specific is to ask yourself *If somebody else read my goal, would they know exactly what I'm trying to do?* Try to revise your goal and make it as specific as possible.

M Is for Measurable

Setting measurable goals allows you to track your progress toward completing the goal. If you don't have a way to measure your goal, how will you ever know if you've accomplished it? When people try to write goals, they often use phrases like "get better" or "improve the quality of," but these are difficult to measure. What does it mean to get better? You want to make sure your goals have outcomes that can be easily measured; that way you'll know when you've accomplished the goal, or how much further you have to go.

How would you measure your goal? To return to our example, if your goal is "Get a B in chemistry," you've already built a measure into the goal. But you could also choose a particular percentage as your measurement—say, "Get an 80% in chemistry"—or you could use test grades as your measurement: "Get a B on each of my chemistry tests." You can also think about how to keep track of your measurement. You could ask your teacher for regular updates on your grade, use your school's online grade book, or wait until you receive your next report card. Waiting for your report card means you won't know how you're doing until you get your result. So waiting for a report card is probably not the best measure, since you can't keep track of it very well. Using your school's online grade book gives you more ability to measure your goal whenever you want to. Ideally, you want your measure to be something you can use or access regularly so you can keep track of your progress. Some common measures include the number of days on which you did something, the amount of time you spent on an activity, or the number of steps you complete in a larger activity or process.

A Is for Attainable

There's no point in setting goals that are impossible to reach! That would just set you up for failure. So it's important to set goals that are realistic. To continue the example, if your goal is "Get a B in chemistry," you need to first ask whether it is *possible* for you to get a B in chemistry. If you are midway through the semester and you currently have a C in chemistry, then improving your grade to a B is probably within reach. If it's two weeks to the semester's end and are currently failing chemistry, then getting a B may no longer be possible. You might need to revise your goal to "Get a passing grade in chemistry." Setting goals that are too difficult or impossible to reach can leave you feeling tired, frustrated, or burned out. On the other hand, if your goals are too easy to reach, you might not get much satisfaction from reaching them. So if you currently have a 79 in chemistry (a C+), setting the goal to get an 80 (a B-) might be attainable, but not particularly satisfying. The ideal goal is enough of a challenge to require effort, but not so challenging that you are tempted to give up! Take a moment to check that your goals are attainable before moving on.

Another part of setting an attainable goal is to figure out the steps needed to reach that goal. Often you can break a goal down into several smaller steps, then complete them one at a time. For example, if you want to get a B in chemistry, what steps will you need to take? One might be to spend a half hour each day studying your chemistry book. Another might be to ask a classmate to tutor you. A third step might be to make some flashcards to study for tests. You might also approach the teacher to ask for assistance or to try to make up any missed assignments. Each of these steps can help you achieve your goal.

Now that you have some steps for reaching your goal, you can check whether each step is attainable. In this case, making flash cards, finding time to study, or asking for help are all probably attainable steps—things you could probably accomplish with a bit of effort. When the steps to achieving your goals are attainable, your overall goal probably is, too.

R Is for Relevant

After all your revising and editing, your goals may look different from how you first defined them. Take a moment to make sure that the goal you have now is still relevant to your original aim. If your goal isn't relevant, if it isn't something that matters to you, then you won't have much desire to accomplish it! You are more likely to succeed if your goals are important to you. Setting goals based on what other people want for you or what you think you *should* do leads to goals that won't hold your interest. Make sure that the goal is still relevant to you and in line with your values and your life goals.

T Is for Time-Bound

Time-bound goals have an end date. Making sure your goals are time-bound helps to ensure that you don't get stuck in an endless loop. Setting a time limit also gives you a push to start working toward your goals right away, instead of always telling yourself *I'll start… tomorrow*. For the goal "Get a B in chemistry," the end date is probably something like "by the end of the semester" or "by the next report card." Even if it feels obvious, be sure to state the end date right in the goal itself. So you could revise your goal to "Get a B in chemistry by the end of the semester." For other goals, the end date might not be as easy to spot. A common type of goal that people set is to spend more time or energy on something, to establish new habits or learn a new skill. These goals often don't have a specific end date, so it can be helpful to create an end date as a way of checking in and reevaluating the goal. For example, for a goal like "Learn to play the guitar" you might decide to "practice playing the guitar for a half hour each day, five days per week, for four weeks." By adding the end date (for four weeks), you give yourself a chance to check in on your progress. Did you practice each of the five days (or most days)? Have you noticed any improvement in your guitar playing skills? Setting an end date—making your goal time-bound—gives you something to work toward. As with setting attainable goals, you want to set an end date that is near enough to realistic, but not so near as to feel rushed!

Setting SMART Goals		
Starting Goal: Do better in school.		
S: Make It Specific		
Add detail. Break it up into smaller goals if needed.	Do better in chemistry.	Do better in history.
M: Make It Measurable.		
Determine **how** to measure it. Add the measurement goal.	Measure with letter grade, check online each week. Aim for a B.	Measure with letter grade, ask teacher to help me track my grade. Aim for a C.
A: Make It Attainable.		
Figure out what steps are needed to reach this goal. Check that those steps are realistic.	Spend a half hour daily studying. Find a tutor. Make flash cards for memorizing things.	Spend a half hour daily studying. Reread the text book after class. Memorize important dates.
R: Make It Relevant.		
Is this goal what you want? Does this align with your original intent (to do better in school)	☐ Yes ☐ No ☐ Yes ☐ No	☐ Yes ☐ No ☐ Yes ☐ No
T: Make It Time-Bound.		
Add an end date.	Get a B in chemistry on my report card at the end of the semester.	Get a C+ in history on my report card at the end of the semester.

Now take a moment to compare your final, revised goal with your original goal. Hopefully, the process of writing a SMART goal has developed your goal into something that you can achieve, with a clear path for success.

You can use the process of creating SMART goals to help you focus on whatever is important to you. You can also use this process to break down big life goals into smaller steps that you can start working on right away.

Take some time to write a few SMART goals based on the things you decided were important to you. Then pick one or two goals to get started on right away. The more you can spend your time and effort on things that are important to you, the more you will build a sense of purpose and direction.

CHOOSE A HEADING AND SET SAIL!

You started this chapter by identifying your reasons for living and determining the things that are most important to you. Then you learned how to turn these things into actionable goals by setting SMART goals. The final step in starting to build a life of purpose is to make plans to act on those goals. Goals are great, but only if they lead to action!

Now it is time to select one (or more) of your SMART goals and start working to accomplish it.

1. Select one of your goals.

2. As a SMART goal, it should be time-bound and have an end date. Put that date into your calendar, planner, or phone.

3. For your SMART goal, you should have identified some steps to take to accomplish that goal. Using your calendar or planner, set some dates or times to complete each of those steps. If they are specific tasks that you'll do once, try to spread them out. If they are things you need

to do many times (like studying a half hour each day), then put them on your to-do list for each day.

4. Now that you know when you'll complete each step, set yourself reminders. Put an alert in your phone or leave yourself a note. Try to make sure you don't forget!

5. Plan for any challenges that might come up. Are there any things that might get in the way of accomplishing your goal? Is there anything that could go wrong? If so, what can you do to overcome those obstacles? Knowing in advance what might go wrong and having a plan can help you better prepare. If you need to, feel free to go back and revise your goals a bit more, to address challenges or obstacles that you think could get in your way.

Now you are all set to start working toward your goals! By selecting goals that are important to you and taking specific steps to reach those goals, you can increase your sense of purpose and direction. Try to do something each day that contributes, even just a tiny bit, toward one of your goals.

PACE YOURSELF

Building a sense of purpose, accomplishing your goals, and making a life worth living is an ongoing process! These things take time. What is important in this chapter is that you start the process. And it may be challenging at first. If it feels daunting, start small. Pick just one reason, one goal, or one plan and then expand. By spending even a little bit of your time and energy on your goals and reasons for living, you'll have less time and energy to focus on thoughts of suicide. Our minds can pay attention to only a limited number of things at one time. So the natural consequence of focusing on your reasons for living is less time and opportunity for your mind to focus on thoughts of suicide. Start small, stick with it, and keep building toward a life you are excited about living.

MOVING FORWARD

In this chapter you focused on strengthening your connection to life and building a sense of purpose and direction. You explored your reasons for living, the relationships that you value, things you want to accomplish, places you want to go, and the impacts you want to have on the world. Then you learned how to use your reasons for living to set goals and begin living in a way that aligns with your beliefs and desires. You learned about setting SMART goals so that you can accomplish the things you want out of life. You've taken several steps toward creating a life with purpose and direction—and building on your desire to live and thrive.

You're nearing the end of this book. In the next chapter, you'll review what you've learned and how far you've come. Then you'll take the exciting step of deciding what comes next!

CHAPTER 8

Where Do I Go from Here?

You made it! You've arrived at the final chapter of this book—but *not* at the final leg of your journey. This chapter is designed to help you look at how far you've come and decide what comes next. First, you'll take stock of where you are now in terms of your thoughts, emotions, and relationships. You'll identify areas where you'd like to continue improving or places you might need additional support. Once you've done that, it's time to look to the future and decide which next steps are right for you. You'll learn about the different types of professional support available and, now that you have some new skills of your own, how to recognize if you might need extra help from a professional. With your options in hand, you'll be prepared to make informed decisions about the next stage of your journey. There are lots more adventures waiting for you!

TIME FOR A CHECKUP

As a young child, you may have gone to the doctor every year for a checkup. The doctor would check your reflexes with a little rubber hammer, measure your height and weight, and listen to your heart and lungs. Doctors recommend a yearly checkup to make sure their patients are staying healthy. A checkup also helps your doctor catch any problems before they become too serious. Similarly, when taking care of your mental health, it is important to do a checkup from time to time. A checkup can give you a sense of how you are doing, identify potential trouble areas, and prompt you to take steps to address any trouble areas before they become big, overwhelming problems.

You know the old saying, "An ounce of prevention is worth a pound of cure?" There's a lot of truth to that statement. Problems often start out small. If we ignore those problems, over time they can become bigger and more complex. Imagine that you get a low grade on some homework. You could ask a classmate or teacher for some additional help, get a tutoring session, or spend extra time studying. On the next homework assignment, you might do better, and your grade doesn't suffer. The problem was a small one and easy to manage. But if you ignore the low grade and don't take steps to correct it, you might get a low grade on the next homework assignment. If you continue to ignore the problem, you might fail the test and get a low grade on your report card. Once you have a low grade, fixing the issue might require lots of make-up work, attending summer school, or retaking the class. See how the problem got bigger, the longer you ignored it? The same is true of lots of things—negative thoughts and emotions, relationship difficulties, and problems at home, school, and work.

A checkup is a quick, useful way to get a sense of how things are going, identify any problem spots, and take steps to correct them. This checkup has two parts. Part 1 focuses on identifying any problem areas or targets for you to actively address. Part 2 focuses on healthy behaviors that help you to maintain good mental health over the long term. The two-part structure is designed to help you get mentally healthy and then stay that way. Unlike your annual checkup with your doctor, though, don't wait an entire year! You're going to keep up on your mental health with monthly checkups. They're quick and easy, as you'll find out in the next section.

Checkup Part 1: How Are Things Going?

To address thoughts of suicide, you've looked at several areas of mental health and well-being throughout this book. Continuing to reduce your thoughts of suicide—or keeping them from coming back—will mean monitoring all these aspects of your mental health. Next, you'll check on each area and use a scale to rate your current state. In your journal, write down each area and your score.

Thoughts of Suicide

In chapter 1 you learned how to measure the intensity of your thoughts of suicide on the scale shown here. Do you remember where your thoughts were on that scale at the start of this book? How would you rate yourself now? Has the intensity of your thoughts of suicide gone down? Even if the *intensity* of your thoughts of suicide hasn't changed, maybe the *frequency* has changed. How often would you say thoughts of suicide have come up for you in the past week? In your journal, make a note of where you are on the scale of suicidal thoughts and how often those thoughts are happening.

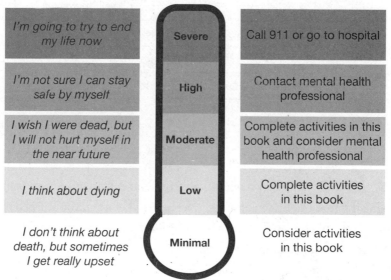

Type of Thoughts	Intensity	Level of Help
I'm going to try to end my life now	Severe	Call 911 or go to hospital
I'm not sure I can stay safe by myself	High	Contact mental health professional
I wish I were dead, but I will not hurt myself in the near future	Moderate	Complete activities in this book and consider mental health professional
I think about dying	Low	Complete activities in this book
I don't think about death, but sometimes I get really upset	Minimal	Consider activities in this book

Safety Planning

In chapter 2 you learned about keeping yourself safe through a technique called safety planning. Have you used your safety plan at all this week? If so, how well did it work? In your notebook, make note of how often you've used your safety plan, and whether or not your safety plan is working well or needs to be revised.

To check in with yourself, you can use this Self Checkup Rating Scale for each of the remaining areas. On this scale, a 0 indicates no problems in a particular area, a 1 or 2 indicates mild to moderate issues, and a 3 or 4 indicates an area you are really struggling with right now.

Self Checkup Rating Scale	
Life Disruption Level	Description
0	No current problems/difficulties in this area.
1	Some minor problems, but I'm coping with them well.
2	Some moderate problems, and I'm struggling to cope.
3	I'm struggling significantly in this area.
4	I'm having major problems; I need help now!

Emotions

In chapter 3 you learned about identifying and managing your feelings. Recognizing that intense emotions can feel overwhelming, you learned about different ways to cope with or manage your emotions, including belly breathing, accepting your emotions, and taking a new perspective. With practice, those skills can help you to manage strong negative emotions. Take a moment to use the Self Checkup Rating Scale again to gauge how much strong emotions have been disrupting your life over the last week. If you've been managing your strong emotions successfully, give yourself a 0. If you've had some difficulties with your feelings and have struggled to manage them or cope with them, give yourself a 1 or 2. If you are really struggling with many strong negative emotions and feel like you can't manage them on your own, give yourself a 3 or 4.

Negative Thoughts

In chapter 4, you learned how negative thoughts can hurt you and how to identify thinking traps, like mind reading, jumping to conclusions, and catastrophizing. You also learned how to talk back to and change negative thoughts. Using the same scale, rate how well you've been managing any negative thoughts that have come up. If you've been talking back to your negative thoughts or if you haven't had many negative thoughts, give yourself a 0. If you've had some negative thoughts and sometimes you've had difficulty managing them, give yourself a 1 or 2. If you are really struggling with negative thoughts and negative self-talk this week, give yourself a 3 or 4.

Stress

In chapter 5 you learned about identifying and managing stress. You learned about how to reduce your stress, boost your mood, and use problem-solving to find solutions. Use the Self Checkup Rating Scale to gauge how you've been managing your stress level over the past week. If you've been managing your stress well, give yourself a 0. If you've had some difficulties managing your stress, give yourself a 1 or 2. If you are really struggling and feeling overwhelmed with stress, give yourself a 3 or 4.

Relationships

In chapter 6 you learned about asking for support, strengthening your existing relationships, and getting out of relationships that might be unhealthy. Again using the Self Checkup Rating Scale, rate how your relationships have been going in the past week. If your relationships have been generally positive and supportive, give yourself a 0. If you've had some arguments or challenges in your relationships, give yourself a 1 or 2. If you are really struggling to maintain your relationships and need lots of support, give yourself a 3 or 4.

Purpose

In chapter 7, you learned about identifying your reasons for living and setting goals to try to live your life with a sense of purpose and direction. Using the same scale, rate how well you've been working toward your goals and focusing on your reasons for living. If you've been working toward your goals or regularly focusing on your reasons for living, give yourself a 0. If you've been ignoring your goals or have struggled to remember your reasons for living, give yourself a 1 or 2. If you are really struggling to find reasons to live, give yourself a 3 or 4.

Interpreting Your Scores

Just like a checkup at the doctor's office, this checkup has a purpose: to identify any areas where action needs to be taken. Now that you've completed your ratings, it's time to evaluate where you are and use what you learn to help guide your next steps.

Take a look back at the scores you gave yourself in Part 1 of the checkup. Areas where you gave yourself a 0 or 1 are places where things are going well for you. If those are areas you have been actively working on, congratulations!

If you've been working hard on a particular area and you've seen improvement, that's great! Keep using your skills and paying attention to this area so that you maintain the progress you've made. You'll probably find that the more you work on an area, the easier it is to maintain your progress. Be sure to keep paying attention to areas where things are going well. When you ignore an area, you are at risk of seeing your progress start to slip. For example, building relationships is hard work and can take lots of time and energy. Once you have a strong relationship, it is important to still give it time and attention, to keep it strong. The same is true of managing your negative thoughts. As you use your skills to challenge or change your negative thoughts, you'll start to feel better. But don't ignore those thoughts in the future—they're sneaky and can creep back in.

For areas where you gave yourself a 2 or 3, revisit the corresponding chapter and practice the skills or techniques introduced in that chapter. For example, if you gave yourself a 3 on your emotions this week, then you've really been struggling to manage strong negative feelings; it would be a good idea to reread the sections on belly breathing, taking a new perspective, and accepting your emotions. You can also set a short-term goal (see chapter 7 on setting SMART goals) focused on practicing skills for managing feelings. A good short-term goal might be "Use an emotion-focused skill every day for two weeks," then check in on how you're feeling.

For any areas where you gave yourself a 4, make that a high-priority area for the next couple of weeks. Revisit the chapter, practice the skills, and make an active effort to address that area. If you have put lots of time and energy into a particular area and still find yourself at a 4, then consider getting help from a professional. Similarly, if you have 3's or 4's in most or all areas, then professional help is a good idea. A professional can teach you additional skills to address the things that are causing difficulty for you. (Of course, each chapter teaches you excellent skills, but there are more skills out there. We couldn't fit every skill into just one book!)

Checkup Part 2: Calculate Your Healthy Habits Score

In each chapter of this book, you worked on new skills or techniques to manage your emotions, change your thoughts, build relationships, or set goals. Often you were asked to practice these skills or work them into your day-to-day life. The purpose of practicing skills is to make them into habits or routines. That way, when challenges arise, you already have the skills you need at the ready.

As you practice skills and make them into regular habits, you may not notice how often you use the healthy skills and habits you've learned. Look at the following score sheet and give yourself a healthy habits score to see how many healthy habits you've adopted. For each behavior you've done in the past week, give yourself the corresponding number of points. If you've done something multiple times, give yourself points for each time you used that healthy habit. Add up your score, then see where you fall on the Healthy Habits Meter that follows.

Healthy Habits	Points
Used my safety plan	5
Was open with others about any thoughts of suicide I had	5
Labeled my emotions	2
Used belly breathing	2
Used one of my mood boosters	3
Identified what I can and can't control	2
Used problem solving	3
Asked someone for support	4
Spent time with someone I cared about	2
Checked whether my relationships were healthy or unhealthy	2
Added something to a memorial	1
Focused on my reasons for living	3
Set a new SMART goal	2
Spent time working toward one of my goals	1
Decatastrophized	2
Avoided jumping to conclusions	2
Acknowledged the positives	2
Ditched double standards	2
Generated positive counterthoughts	2

Interpreting Your Healthy Habits Score

What was your healthy habits score for this past week? Was it higher or lower than you expected? See how your score stacks up.

Healthy Habits Meter		
27+	*Amazing!*	**My healthy habits score was greater than 20:** Congratulations! You've been regularly using a variety of skills to keep yourself safe, manage your thoughts and emotions, and build strong relationships. Keep it going as you turn these skills into habits.
24–27	*Excellent!*	
21–23	*Great!*	
18–20	*Going strong!*	**My healthy habits score was between 11 and 20:** Nicely done! You've started using several skills throughout the week (or one skill quite a lot). Keep up the good work! Try to add one or two more skills this week, to keep raising your healthy habits score. Consistency is key—making these skills into habits will pay off in the long run.
14–17	*Looking good*	
11–13	*Getting there*	
8–10	*Making an effort*	**My healthy habits score was less than 11:** Keep working to use the various skills and techniques you learned in this book. Practice, practice, practice! Making these skills into habits will help improve your emotional well-being and reduce the intensity of your suicidal thoughts. If you need to, revisit previous chapters to brush up on how to use the different skills.
4–7	*Getting into gear*	
0–3	*Just starting out*	

If your healthy habits score was on the low end of the scale, find one skill to practice over the next week, to start building up your healthy habits score a bit at a time. By focusing on one new skill each week, you can practice several times and start to establish them as habits. If your healthy habits score was somewhere in the middle, then you've already started using some skills from the earlier chapters. Continue to develop new skills over the next few weeks. Revisit your scores from the checkup and select an area to target, then select a skill from the corresponding chapter. Practice it throughout the week to keep improving your skill set. If your healthy habits score was on the high end of the scale, you're already using lots of skills. Keep using those skills so that they become habits—things you do without even thinking about it. By making these skills into habits, you'll find that using skills gets easier and doesn't take as much effort and energy.

Now take a moment to imagine that things are going perfectly in every area of your life. You have no thoughts of suicide, your thoughts and feelings are positive, your stress level is low, and you have strong relationships and a strong sense of purpose in your life. What a wonderful world that would be! Even if all of those things were true, it would *still* be a good idea to use and practice some of the skills you learned in the previous chapters. You might work toward or check in on your goals, label your emotions, and continue to strengthen your relationships. The point is, no matter how well things are going, these skills really are healthy habits—things you can do to keep yourself healthy every day.

LOOK AT HOW FAR YOU'VE COME!

Sometimes it's important to look back at where you've been, so you can see how far you've come. When you make changes little by little or work toward big goals step by step, sometimes you don't notice how much progress you've really made. It's a sort of trick of the mind that we don't notice small changes over time in the same way that we notice big, sudden changes. Have you ever looked in the mirror and thought *Oh wow, I really need a haircut?* Your hair usually grows about a half inch per month, which is slow enough that you may not notice how long it has gotten until you notice it all at once. Gradual changes can go unnoticed, but when they are the result of hard work—like changes you've made over the course of this book—they deserve to be noticed, appreciated, and celebrated.

What changes have you noticed as you've progressed on your journey? Have you:

- Learned a new skill or practiced a new technique?

- Set a SMART goal and worked to achieve it?

- Labeled more of your emotions or coped with a strong emotion?

- Noticed an unhelpful thought and changed it to a more positive one?

- Formed a new relationship or strengthened an existing one?

Each of these little victories *is* a victory! Big changes happen when you add up lots of small changes.

CELEBRATE YOUR PROGRESS

As you look back at the changes you've made throughout your journey and all the healthy habits and skills you've adopted, you should take time to celebrate the progress you've made. You don't have to wait until your life is Instagram perfect to celebrate progress. Instead, you should celebrate small signs of change. Did you have a good day, get yourself through a crisis, or successfully ask for help or support when you needed it? Using your skills in day-to-day situations is where real change happens, so celebrate those wins.

Celebrating little victories has two purposes. First, it's important to recognize that you've used your skills or made progress toward your goals. Taking care of your mental health is difficult! Celebrating your progress is a way of reminding yourself that you are doing something challenging and worthwhile—and it forces you to stop and take note of the changes you *have* made. Celebrating progress, even though the larger journey may be just getting started, can help keep you motivated when the going gets tough.

The second reason to celebrate is this: Celebrating is fun! Thoughts of suicide often occur when you feel worthless or depressed, lose interest in things, or struggle to find joy in anything. Taking time to celebrate and reward yourself is a good way to also help combat those feelings. Every little bit of joy and celebration can help.

So how do you like to celebrate? What feels good to you? Some people like to share their victories with others, either in person or on social media. Others like to take time for themselves—like reserving an evening for an at-home spa day, complete with bubble bath, face mask, and a candle or two. Maybe you like to treat yourself to a movie night, a snack from your favorite bakery, or a latte at your favorite café.

Take a few minutes to create a menu of rewards in your notebook. Try to list three to five things that you can use to reward yourself for making progress. If you get stuck, look at the rewards menu list for some ideas, or look back at your mood boosters from chapter 5. Then select one and celebrate how far you've come.

My Rewards Menu

Share with a friend and celebrate.

Give myself a manicure or pedicure.

Create a "spa day" at home–hot bath, bubbles, candles, the works.

Watch my favorite movie, with popcorn.

Get a fancy coffee or hot chocolate.

Get my favorite treat–or, better yet, make it.

Go to the park on a nice day.

Spend an hour or two on my favorite activity.

Curl up with my favorite book and a cup of tea.

WHAT COMES NEXT?

You've been working hard to learn new skills for managing your thoughts of suicide and to address some of the common drivers of suicidal thoughts (negative emotions, stress, relationship difficulties, and negative thoughts). As you continue to practice and master the skills you've learned in your journey, it's a good idea to look at the road ahead and plan a route for the future. In this section, you'll learn about a few different paths for the next stage of your journey. Knowing your options can help you decide which path is best for you right now.

Path #1: Stick to the Road You're On

One option is to stick to the path you've been on throughout this book. This includes continuing to practice and master the skills you've learned in the previous chapters, managing your thoughts of suicide, using your safety plan, managing your feelings, keeping your stress in check, building your relationships, living with purpose, setting goals, and challenging negative thoughts.

If you've been making good progress so far, then sticking to your current path is a good option for you. If you choose Path #1, be sure to schedule checkups at least once a month, continue to build on the skills you've learned, and work to raise your healthy habits score.

Path #2: Seek Out a Stronger Support Team

A second option is to consider getting some assistance in the form of professional mental health care. While the skills and techniques in this book can help young people manage and reduce thoughts of suicide, some will require a bit of extra help. There's no shame in seeking that help. Engaging the support of a mental health care professional is a great way to get extra support and assistance in dealing with thoughts of suicide.

At certain points in your life, you've needed a doctor's care. Whether it was a trip to the emergency room for a broken bone, an urgent care clinic for a bad flu, or your primary care doctor for a shot, antibiotics, or a physical, you've likely interacted with the healthcare system. And you probably didn't worry that visiting a doctor or hospital was unusual or that it might mean there was something "wrong" with you. Yet when it comes to getting care for our mental health, too often there is still a stigma attached. Many people worry that seeing a mental health care provider means they are crazy or that something is wrong with them. You might worry that others will view you differently. It might also seem scary because you don't know what is going to happen. You might not know what mental health care looks like—or you might not know where to start.

Imagine for a moment that your friend Stella tells you that she has been having terrible headaches a couple of times each week for the past few months. When she has these headaches, she can't think clearly, she can't focus on anything, and she needs to be in a very quiet, dark room, because noise and light are painful. Stella shares that her headaches have gotten so bad that she can't keep up in school and her grades are starting to suffer. She hasn't been spending time with her friends and family, and she has stopped doing many of her hobbies, because she can't find the time. Stella says she has tried over-the-counter headache medicines, but those haven't worked. She confesses that she doesn't know what to do! What suggestions might you give to Stella?

You might recognize these headaches as migraines. Migraines are a fairly common problem. They can be quite serious and require treatment from a doctor. Untreated, migraines are painful and can really mess with your life. You would probably suggest that Stella see her doctor (or get her parents to take her to a doctor). The doctor can probably figure out what is causing them and get Stella whatever treatment she needs.

In the same way that migraines are a sign of a medical problem that needs to be addressed, thoughts of suicide are a sign of a mental health problem that needs to be addressed. You can start by trying to treat it yourself, by using the skills you learned in this book. But if that isn't enough, it is important to see a health care professional. In the case of thoughts of suicide, that would be someone who specializes in mental health. While many people have a doctor they see for checkups or physical health issues, most people don't have a regular mental health professional to see when the need arises. Mental health care is just as important as physical health care. But finding the right care can be a challenge. The next section will help you navigate the options.

Is Professional Help Right for Me? Understand Your Options

Many people can benefit from professional mental health care, but finding the right type of care can be challenging. There are lots of different types of providers and approaches to therapy—and this isn't something you usually learn about in school. As you consider whether mental health care might be right for you, take some time to learn about the different types of care that might be available to you. Here are the most common types of treatment:

- *Psychosocial therapy,* also called *talk therapy,* involves learning skills to manage your thoughts and feelings on your own. You may work on improving your relationships, managing your thoughts, coping with your emotions, managing stress, or learning other skills and techniques. It's a bit like having a personal coach to help you make progress.

- *Medication therapy* involves taking medicine, like antidepressant medications to help improve your mood. Medications are typically prescribed by a psychiatrist but may sometimes be prescribed by your primary care physician.

- *Combination therapy* involves both medication and psychosocial therapy. The medication can help to manage your mood while you learn new skills in therapy. In some cases, combination therapy can be more effective than either medication or psychosocial therapy alone.

There are also different types of providers with different roles:

- *Psychiatrists* are medical doctors who specialize in mental health concerns. As medical doctors, they can prescribe medications. Typically, psychiatrists focus on using medication-based treatments for mental health concerns. Some may also offer psychosocial therapy.

- *Psychologists* are licensed professionals who provide psychosocial therapy. Psychologists often focus on teaching you skills for managing your thoughts and feelings and for strengthening your relationships. Psychologists also have the title of doctor, but their degree is in psychology instead of medicine. Generally, psychologists do *not* prescribe medications.

- *Psychological associates, professional counselors, social workers, and therapists* are also licensed professionals who may provide psychosocial therapy. Like psychologists, they often focus on teaching you skills for managing your thoughts and feelings and for strengthening your relationships.

As you can see, there are a lot of options! Knowing what different types of services exist can help you determine which you would prefer. For example, some people have a strong dislike for taking medication. If that's you, then a psychiatrist, who typically provides medication-based treatments, is probably *not* the best fit. Instead, you might seek out a psychologist or other therapist for psychosocial therapy.

What Therapy Looks Like

If you've decided you'd like to go with Path #2 and seek some extra help, · you may be wondering what happens next. Going into the unknown can be a scary experience! The more you know ahead of time, the more comfortable you are likely to feel during your first visit. So, what are the steps involved? And what does therapy actually look like?

The first step is to get an appointment. It's likely that a caregiver will need to do this for you. They will select a provider or clinic or get a referral from your family doctor. If you have health insurance, your plan may offer a limited selection of in-network providers. Depending on where you live, there may be a waitlist to see a provider. These waitlists can be several weeks or even months long. That said, if you are having thoughts of suicide, it is important to let the provider know that when you approach them to schedule an appointment. For safety reasons, a clinic may wish to prioritize getting you in quickly or may recommend that you try another clinic with a shorter waiting period. (Pro tip: If you have flexibility, ask the clinic to put you on the waitlist and let you know if they get a cancellation. Providers don't like to have gaps in their schedules, so if you can attend a visit on short notice, they might get you in sooner!) Also, many professionals now offer telehealth options, where sessions happen using video chat. It may be easier to find a provider who is located farther away from you but who offers telehealth.

When you arrive at your first appointment, you'll typically start by talking through everything that is going on, to find the best treatment for your situation. This will usually include the providers making a diagnosis—or naming a specific condition or disorder for which you meet criteria. Diagnoses put a label on how you are thinking, feeling, and acting. That label helps professionals find the best treatment options for you. Most of the time, a diagnosis is also necessary for your provider to submit a bill for your session. Just remember, a diagnosis is *not* a judgment about you and doesn't mean that you are crazy or that there is anything wrong with you. Diagnoses are just labels to help point providers in the right direction.

Once you have your diagnosis and treatment plan, you can begin therapy. How often you visit your provider typically depends on the type of treatment you are receiving. For psychosocial therapy, a typical schedule is a weekly one-hour treatment session. The duration of therapy varies widely based on the selected treatment, but typically lasts for, at minimum, twelve to sixteen weeks. For medication-based treatments, you'll likely have regular short visits with a psychiatrist to oversee your prescriptions and your response to them.

In the event your thoughts of suicide become extremely intense and your provider is worried for your safety, they may recommend *psychiatric hospitalization*. Just like a regular hospital, a psychiatric hospital will admit you, meaning that you stay at the hospital for a short time. Typically, psychiatric hospitalization lasts for a few days to a week. It often involves a combination of medications and psychosocial therapy, and it is intended as a safe space for you during a crisis. Often there are rules about access to your phone, the types of clothing you can wear (such as not having shoelaces or belts), and when you can have visitors. These rules are designed to keep you, and the other patients, safe from harm.

How to Get the Most Out of Therapy

If you choose to begin therapy, here are a few tips for getting the most out of the experience:

- Attend regularly. Therapy requires a degree of trust and comfort between you and your therapist. Attending weekly sessions is key to establishing that relationship. If you don't feel comfortable with your therapist, you will probably find it harder to share your thoughts and feelings in therapy. Once you're established as a patient, regular sessions are key to making steady progress.

- Be open and honest about your thoughts and feelings. Developing a good relationship with your therapist requires being honest even when it is uncomfortable. It's a challenge to step outside of your comfort zone, but it can help you progress in your journey.

- Practice skills between sessions. Many of the skills learned in psychosocial therapy take time and practice to be effective. As is true of many of the skills and techniques you learned in this book, consistent effort turns new skills into healthy habits. And as with learning any new skills, consistency is key.

- For medication therapy, it is important to carefully follow your doctor's instructions. Set reminders to avoid missing doses, and *always* seek medical advice before skipping doses or stopping any medication.

PICK YOUR PATH—AND CONTINUE YOUR JOURNEY

Now that you've had a chance to learn your options for the next leg of your journey, it's time to determine which path you will follow. How do you know which path is best?

Look back at the results of your checkup at the start of this chapter. In Checkup Part 1 you rated your suicidal thoughts as *minimal, low, moderate, high,* or *severe.* If you rated your suicidal thoughts as *high* or *severe,* then we strongly recommend Path #2. If you've been working on the skills and techniques you learned in this book and your suicidal thoughts are still at *moderate,* you can continue practicing and implementing these skills and follow Path #1, or you may also wish to pursue Path #2 and seek a higher level of support. In Checkup Part 1 you also rated your current challenges in each of the areas targeted in the previous chapters, on a scale from 0 (*no problems*) to 4 (*major problems*). If your ratings included several 3 or 4 ratings, then you can continue or resume using the skills in this book and follow Path #1. But if you feel like you're getting stuck and not making progress on your own, Path #2 may be a good fit for you. If your current suicidal thoughts were rated as *none* or *low,* and if your current challenges were ranked mostly 0, 1 or 2, with only a couple at 3 and 4, then Path #1, continuing to practice the skills you learned in this book may be all you need.

In addition to reviewing your checkup, you should certainly discuss your options with a trusted adult. That could be a parent, grandparent, aunt or uncle, a counselor at school, a faith leader, or your physician. (If you need someone to support you or to provide advice, revisit chapter 6 to learn more about seeking support.) Once you've done that and thought carefully about what you want and need, it's time to decide what comes next for you. Of course, you can always change your mind later, so don't worry about making the wrong choice.

Once you've decided what comes next for you, take action! If you selected Path #1 ("stick to the road you're on"), you should plan to revisit the skills you've learned here, schedule regular checkups, and keep practicing your healthy habits. If you selected Path #2 ("seek out a stronger support team"), plan to contact a mental health professional and arrange your first session. Capitalize on the momentum you've built and all of your hard work so far to keep making progress. Either option, Path #1 or Path #2, can lead to a happier, healthier you.

A Final Note from the Authors

Dear Reader,

We sincerely hope that your journey through this book has been helpful to you. We recognize that it was challenging, even overwhelming, at times. Change is hard. Staying motivated is hard. Keeping up hope when the world seems terrible is hard. But you are strong, probably much stronger than you know. Making the effort to read this book, to try the skills, to continue fighting when you have thoughts of suicide takes tremendous strength.

We have worked with many young people from a wide range of backgrounds and with different life experiences and circumstances. We have seen people struggle with thoughts of suicide and the desire to harm themselves. We have seen these same people go on to lead healthy, fulfilling lives. When we say there is hope, we speak from having seen others fight these same fights. Living isn't easy, but it is so, so worth fighting for.

So keep fighting to live. Keep fighting to overcome suicidal thoughts—and all of the negative thoughts and uncomfortable emotions that come with them. *There is hope.*

And go easy on yourself. You are doing the best you can, at this moment. If trying a new skill is too much for you today, then use a skill you already have. If it's a fight to get out of bed today, then getting out of bed counts as a victory. Keep doing your best—and don't be afraid to ask for help when you need it. Fighting to live is one fight you shouldn't face alone.

Always remember that you can revisit these pages whenever you need a new skill to practice or want to refresh your memory of an existing skill. Nobody masters a new skill on the first try, so revisit these chapters often and use them as a guide for managing your feelings, coping with stress, challenging negative thoughts, setting goals, and seeking support.

Finally, as you continue on your journey, be sure to celebrate and share your progress with the world. In the fight against suicidal thoughts, living *is* a victory. And every victory is worth celebrating. The world is better with you in it.

Someday we will create a world where nobody need ever consider suicide. We aren't there yet, but we'll do it, with your help. Your strength is our inspiration.

Best wishes on your journey,

Jeremy and Ryan

Resources

The National Suicide Prevention Lifeline is available 24/7 to provide support. Call 988. Trained professionals are available to help you if a crisis arises. You can also visit their website at www.suicidepreventionlifeline.org. Their website also offers chat services for those who are deaf or hard of hearing and a line for assistance and support in Spanish.

The Crisis Text Line offers text message–based support in times of crisis. Text the message "home" to the number 741741 any time, day or night. Visit their website at www.crisistextline.org. Their website includes helpful information as well as a link to their WhatsApp chat option.

The Trevor Project offers online resources for LGBTQ people. Their website, www.thetrevorproject.org, offers a live chat feature, available 24/7. They also have a telephone hotline (call 1-866-488-7386) and a text message hotline (text "START" to 678678).

To learn more about suicide and suicide prevention, visit the website of the American Foundation for Suicide Prevention at www.afsp.org.

References

Brent, D. A., Poling, K. D., & Goldstein, T. R. (2011). *Treating depressed and suicidal adolescents: A clinician's guide*. Guilford Press.

Curry, J. F., Wells, K. C., Brent, D. A., Clarke, G. N., Rohde, P., Albano, A. M., Reinecke, M. A., Benazon, N., & March, J. S. (2005). *Treatment for adolescents with depression study (TADS) cognitive behavior therapy manual: Introduction, rationale, and adolescent sessions*. Duke University Medical Center.

Grover, K. E., Green, K. L., Pettit, J. W., Garza, M. J., Monteith, L. L., & Venta, A. (2009). Problem-solving moderates the effects of life event and chronic stress on suicidal behaviors in adolescence. *Journal of Clinical Psychology, 65*(12), 1281–1290.

Hill, R. M., Dodd, C. G., Do, C., Gomez, M., & Kaplow, J. B. (2020). The Safety Planning Assistant: Feasibility and acceptability of a web-based suicide safety planning tool for at-risk adolescents and their parents. *Evidence-Based Practice in Child and Adolescent Mental Health, 5*(2), 164–172. 10.1080/23794925.2020.1759469

Hill, R. M., Oosterhoff, B., Layne, C. M., Rooney, E., Yudovich, S., Pynoos, R. S., & Kaplow, J. B. (2019). Multidimensional grief therapy: An open trial of a novel intervention for bereaved children and adolescents. *Journal of Child and Family Studies, 28*, 3062–3074. 10.1007/s10826 -019-01481-x

Interagency Working Group on Youth Programs. (n.d.). Characteristics of healthy & unhealthy relationships. Youth.gov. https://youth.gov/youth -topics/teen-dating-violence/characteristics

Ivey-Stephenson, A. Z., Demissie, Z., Crosby, A. E., et al. (2020). Suicidal ideation and behaviors among high school students—Youth Risk Behavior Survey, United States, 2019. *Morbidity and Mortality Weekly Report* (MMWR) Supplement 2020, 69(Suppl-1), 47–55.

Joiner, T. E., Jr. (2005). *Why people die by suicide.* Harvard University Press.

National Domestic Violence Hotline. (2021). Warning signs of abuse. National Domestic Violence Hotline. https://www.thehotline.org /identify-abuse/domestic-abuse-warning-signs/

Planned Parenthood Federation of America Inc. (2021). Abusive relationships. Planned Parenthood. https://www.plannedparenthood .org/learn/teens/relationships/abusive-relationships

Stanley, B., & Brown, G. (2012). Safety planning intervention: A brief intervention to mitigate suicide risk. *Cognitive and Behavioral Practice, 19*(2), 256–264. https://doi.org/10.1016/j.cbpra.2011.01.001

Substance Abuse and Mental Health Services Administration. (2020). *Key substance use and mental health indicators in the United States: Results from the 2019 National Survey on Drug Use and Health* (HHS Publication No. PEP20-07-01-001, NSDUH Series H-55). Center for Behavioral Health Statistics and Quality, Substance Abuse and Mental Health Services Administration. https://www.samhsa.gov/data/

Suicide Prevention Resource Center. (n.d.). CALM: Counseling on access to lethal means. Substance Abuse and Mental Health Services Administration. https://www.sprc.org/resources-programs/calm -counseling-access-lethal-means

Jeremy W. Pettit, PhD, is professor of psychology and psychiatry at Florida International University. A licensed psychologist, his clinical research program focuses on the etiology and treatment of anxiety, depression, and suicidal behaviors. He has published more than 150 scholarly works on these topics and received multiple awards for his work, including the Edwin Shneidman Award from the American Association of Suicidology (AAS), and the Self-Help Book of Merit Award from the Association for Behavioral and Cognitive Therapies.

Ryan M. Hill, PhD, is a psychologist and assistant professor of psychology at the University of Texas at San Antonio. He is a member of the AAS, and has published more than sixty scholarly works on suicide prevention and child and adolescent mental health.

More ⏱Instant Help Books for Teens